16

STUDY GUIDE

Changes in Medicine, c1848–c1948

Edexcel - IGCSE

app
available

Mrs L Ashley
2 Kingston Bay Road
SHOREHAM-BY-SEA
BN43 5HP

Published by Clever Lili Limited.

contact@cleverlili.com

First published 2020

ISBN 978-1-913887-15-5

Contributors: Emily Bishop, James George, Rebecca Lawrence, Lynn Harkin, Marcus Pailing, Jen Mellors

Edited by Paul Connolly and Rebecca Parsley

Design by Evgeni Veskov and Will Fox

DISCOVER MORE OF OUR IGCSE HISTORY STUDY GUIDES

GCSEHistory.com and Clever Lili

X

Edexcel - IGCSE

STUDY GUIDE

Germany:
Development of Dictatorship, 1918-45

GCSEHistory.com

Edexcel - IGCSE

STUDY GUIDE

A World Divided: Superpower Relations, 1943-72

GCSEHistory.com

Edexcel - IGCSE

STUDY GUIDE

Russia and the Soviet Union, 1905-24

GCSEHistory.com

Edexcel - IGCSE

STUDY GUIDE

Dictatorship and Conflict in the USSR, 1924-53

GCSEHistory.com

Edexcel - IGCSE

STUDY GUIDE

The Origins and Course of the First World War, 1905-18

GCSEHistory.com

Edexcel - IGCSE

STUDY GUIDE

The Vietnam Conflict, 1945-75

GCSEHistory.com

Edexcel - IGCSE

STUDY GUIDE

A Divided Union: Civil Rights in the USA, 1945-74

GCSEHistory.com

Edexcel - IGCSE

STUDY GUIDE

The USA, 1918-41

GCSEHistory.com

Edexcel - IGCSE

STUDY GUIDE

China: Conflict, Crisis and Change, 1900-89

GCSEHistory.com

Contents

Quizzes, amazing exam preparation tools and more at GCSEHistory.com

The Birth of the NHS

In this study guide, you will see a series of icons, highlighted words and page references. The key below will help you quickly establish what these mean and where to go for more information.

Icons

 WHAT questions cover the key events and themes.

WHO questions cover the key people involved.

WHEN questions cover the timings of key events.

WHERE questions cover the locations of key moments.

WHY questions cover the reasons behind key events.

HOW questions take a closer look at the way in which events, situations and trends occur.

IMPORTANCE questions take a closer look at the significance of events, situations, and recurrent trends and themes.

DECISIONS questions take a closer look at choices made at events and situations during this era.

Highlighted words

Abdicate - occasionally, you will see certain words highlighted within an answer. This means that, if you need it, you'll find an explanation of the word or phrase in the glossary which starts on **page 76**.

Page references

Tudor *(p. 7)* - occasionally, a certain subject within an answer is covered in more depth on a different page. If you'd like to learn more about it, you can go directly to the page indicated.

Changes in Medicine c1848 - c1948 is an Edexcel iGCSE Breadth Study. It covers the changes in and development of medicine in Britain from the Public Health Act of 1848 to the beginning of the National Health Service, examining developments in medical knowledge, surgery, nursing, treatment and public health, as well as the impact of the world wars.

Purpose

This course allows you to understand the nature, extend and process of change in medicine. You will be able to identify the key features and characteristics of medicine in this time period, and develop the ability to explain, analyse and make judgements about the developments in medicine during this time.

Enquiries

The course is split into the following enquiries:

- The development of nursing, including the role of Florence Nightingale and the impact of women in nursing during the world wars.
- Surgical advances, including Lister and the development of aseptic surgical practices, anaesthetics, Simpson and the discovery of chloroform, Landsteiner and the development of blood transfusions and surgical practices in the world wars.
- Developments in public health, including the work of Chadwick, the Public Health Acts of 1848 and 1875, the impact of industrial cities on health, cholera and the work of John Snow, the Liberal reforms of 1906 and the introduction of the NHS.
- Improving medical knowledge. This includes the work of Pasteur and Koch on germ theory, the development of Magic Bullets, the discovery of penicillin and the work of Fleming, Florey and Chain.
- The impact of the world wars on medicine, including the challenges of trench warfare and advances in medical understanding, surgical practices, and nursing,

Key Individuals

The following key individuals are covered in this course:

- Edwin Chadwick.
- James Simpson.
- Joseph Lister.
- Louis Pasteur.
- Robert Koch.
- Paul Ehrlich.
- Karl Landsteiner.
- Harold Gillies.
- Harvey Cushing.
- Alexander Fleming.
- Howard Florey.
- Ernst Chain.
- Archibald McIndoe.
- Dwight Harken.
- Wylie McKissock.

Assessment

This unit is assessed on Paper 2 Section B. The paper contains three questions.

- Question (a) is worth 6 marks. It will ask you to explain two differences or similarities across the time period. You must use specific details from each example to fully explain the similarities or differences.
- Question (b) is worth 8 marks. It will ask you to explain two causes or consequences of an event. You must use accurate, relevant and detailed historical facts to show how each cause led to the event, or how each consequence resulted from it.

Question (c) is worth 16 marks, and you will have a choice of one of two questions. It will ask you to make a judgement about 'how far' a historical statement is true. You must select at least three points to support your answer, use accurate, relevant and detailed knowledge to explain and analyse whether they support the statement, and reach a judgement based on the points that you have made. The question will give you two bullet points to help you to answer, but you must use at least one more of your own.

Revision! A dreaded word. Everyone knows it's coming, everyone knows how much it helps with your exam performance, and everyone struggles to get started! We know you want to do the best you can in your IGCSEs, but schools aren't always clear on the best way to revise. This can leave students wondering:

✓ How should I plan my revision time?

✓ How can I beat procrastination?

✓ What methods should I use? Flash cards? Re-reading my notes? Highlighting?

Luckily, you no longer need to guess at the answers. Education researchers have looked at all the available revision studies, and the jury is in. They've come up with some key pointers on the best ways to revise, as well as some thoughts on popular revision methods that aren't so helpful. The next few pages will help you understand what we know about the best revision methods.

How can I beat procrastination?

This is an age-old question, and it applies to adults as well! Have a look at our top three tips below.

◎ Reward yourself

When we think a task we have to do is going to be boring, hard or uncomfortable, we often put if off and do something more 'fun' instead. But we often don't really enjoy the 'fun' activity because we feel guilty about avoiding what we should be doing. Instead, get your work done and promise yourself a reward after you complete it. Whatever treat you choose will seem all the sweeter, and you'll feel proud for doing something you found difficult. Just do it!

◎ Just do it!

We tend to procrastinate when we think the task we have to do is going to be difficult or dull. The funny thing is, the most uncomfortable part is usually making ourselves sit down and start it in the first place. Once you begin, it's usually not nearly as bad as you anticipated.

◎ Pomodoro technique

The pomodoro technique helps you trick your brain by telling it you only have to focus for a short time. Set a timer for 20 minutes and focus that whole period on your revision. Turn off your phone, clear your desk, and work. At the end of the 20 minutes, you get to take a break for five. Then, do another 20 minutes. You'll usually find your rhythm and it becomes easier to carry on because it's only for a short, defined chunk of time.

Spaced practice

We tend to arrange our revision into big blocks. For example, you might tell yourself: "This week I'll do all my revision for the Cold War, then next week I'll do the Medicine Through Time unit."

This is called **massed practice**, because all revision for a single topic is done as one big mass.

But there's a better way! Try **spaced practice** instead. Instead of putting all revision sessions for one topic into a single block, space them out. See the example below for how it works.

This means planning ahead, rather than leaving revision to the last minute - but the evidence strongly suggests it's worth it. You'll remember much more from your revision if you use **spaced practice** rather than organising it into big blocks. Whichever method you choose, though, remember to reward yourself with breaks.

Spaced practice (more effective):

week 1	week 2	week 3	week 4
Topic 1	Topic 1	Topic 1	Topic 1
Topic 2	Topic 2	Topic 2	Topic 2
Topic 3	Topic 3	Topic 3	Topic 3
Topic 4	Topic 4	Topic 4	Topic 4

Massed practice (less effective)

week 1	week 2	week 3	week 4
Topic 1	Topic 2	Topic 3	Topic 4

Quizzes, amazing exam preparation tools and more at GCSEHistory.com

What methods should I use to revise?

Self-testing/flash cards

Self explanation/mind-mapping

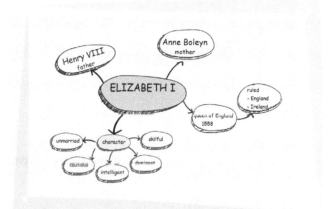

The research shows a clear winner for revision methods - **self-testing**. A good way to do this is with **flash cards**. Flash cards are really useful for helping you recall short – but important – pieces of information, like names and dates.

When was the Yalta Conference?

Side A - question

February 1945

Side B - answer

Write questions on one side of the cards, and the answers on the back. This makes answering the questions and then testing yourself easy. Put all the cards you get right in a pile to one side, and only repeat the test with the ones you got wrong - this will force you to work on your weaker areas.

pile with right answers

pile with wrong answers

As this book has a quiz question structure itself, you can use it for this technique.

Another good revision method is **self-explanation**. This is where you explain how and why one piece of information from your course linked with another piece.

This can be done with **mind-maps**, where you draw the links and then write explanations for how they connect. For example, President Truman is connected with anti-communism because of the Truman Doctrine.

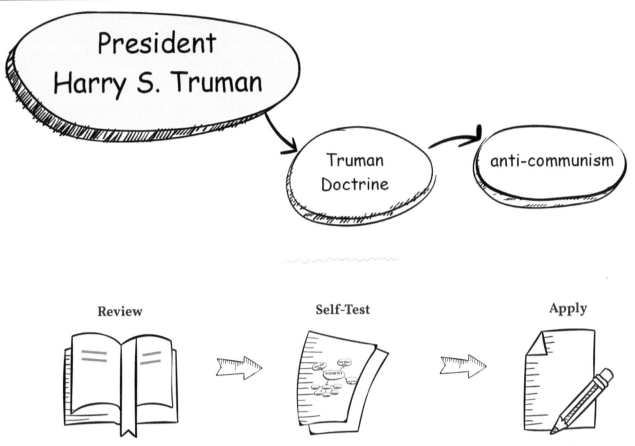

Review	Self-Test	Apply
Start by highlighting or re-reading to create your flashcards for self-testing.	Test yourself with flash cards. Make mind maps to explain the concepts.	Apply your knowledge on practice exam questions.

Which revision techniques should I be cautious about?

Highlighting and **re-reading** are not necessarily bad strategies - but the research does say they're less effective than flash cards and mind-maps.

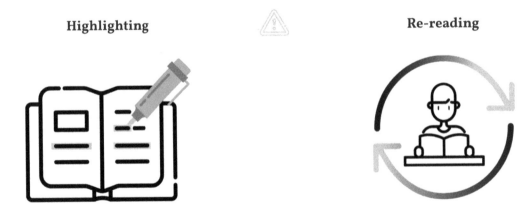

If you do use these methods, make sure they are **the first step to creating flash cards**. Really engage with the material as you go, rather than switching to autopilot.

Quizzes, amazing exam preparation tools and more at GCSEHistory.com

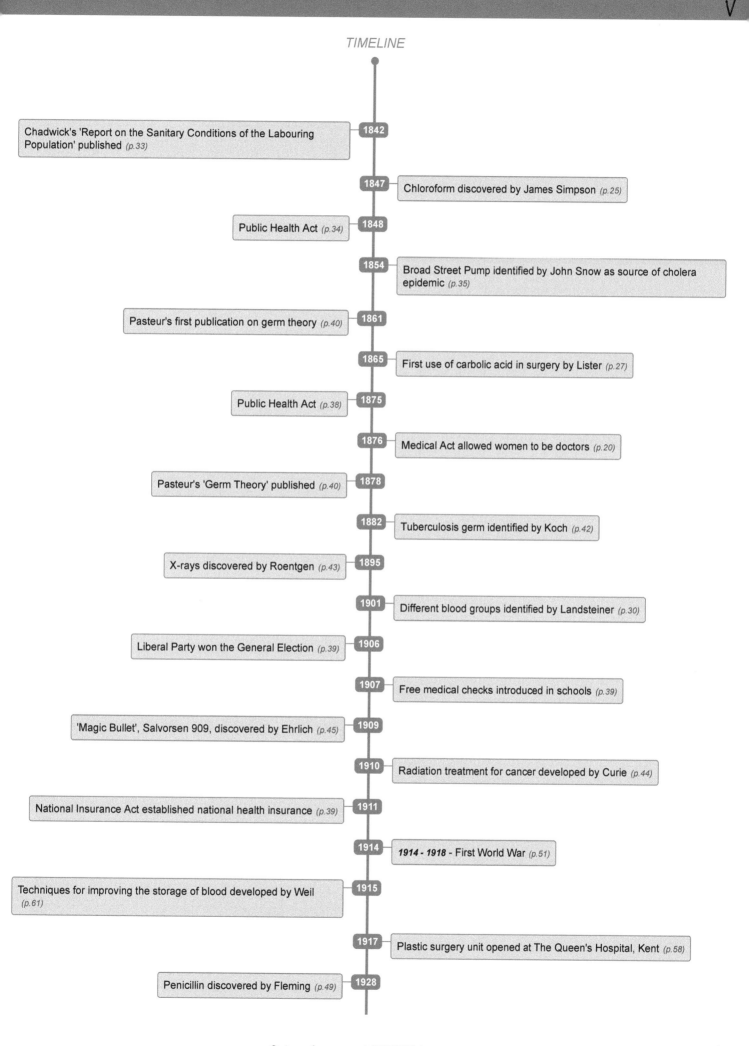

TIMELINE

1842 Chadwick's 'Report on the Sanitary Conditions of the Labouring Population' published *(p.33)*

1847 Chloroform discovered by James Simpson *(p.25)*

1848 Public Health Act *(p.34)*

1854 Broad Street Pump identified by John Snow as source of cholera epidemic *(p.35)*

1861 Pasteur's first publication on germ theory *(p.40)*

1865 First use of carbolic acid in surgery by Lister *(p.27)*

1875 Public Health Act *(p.38)*

1876 Medical Act allowed women to be doctors *(p.20)*

1878 Pasteur's 'Germ Theory' published *(p.40)*

1882 Tuberculosis germ identified by Koch *(p.42)*

1895 X-rays discovered by Roentgen *(p.43)*

1901 Different blood groups identified by Landsteiner *(p.30)*

1906 Liberal Party won the General Election *(p.39)*

1907 Free medical checks introduced in schools *(p.39)*

1909 'Magic Bullet', Salvorsen 909, discovered by Ehrlich *(p.45)*

1910 Radiation treatment for cancer developed by Curie *(p.44)*

1911 National Insurance Act established national health insurance *(p.39)*

1914 *1914 - 1918* - First World War *(p.51)*

1915 Techniques for improving the storage of blood developed by Weil *(p.61)*

1917 Plastic surgery unit opened at The Queen's Hospital, Kent *(p.58)*

1928 Penicillin discovered by Fleming *(p.49)*

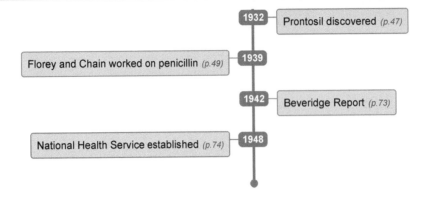

1932 Prontosil discovered *(p.47)*

Florey and Chain worked on penicillin *(p.49)* **1939**

1942 Beveridge Report *(p.73)*

National Health Service established *(p.74)* **1948**

MEDICINE BEFORE 1848

Slow progress in medical understanding for centuries

 What was medicine like before 1848?

For hundreds of years before 1848 *(p.34)*, progress in medical knowledge had been very slow.

Why didn't medicine progress much before 1848?

There were a number of reasons why medical knowledge took a long time to progress before 1848 *(p.34)*.

☑ Medical knowledge was based on ideas which were ultimately wrong, but which seemed rational and logical to people at the time.

☑ Scientists weren't very clear about anatomy and how the human body worked.

☑ People, including doctors and their patients, preferred to stick to their traditional ways of doing things.

☑ The technology used to make discoveries took a long time to develop.

☑ Some people and institutions - for example the medieval Church - benefitted from controlling the level of understanding around health.

☑ Nobody took responsibility for funding and encouraging research. The government did not see it as its business.

 What medical theories did they have before 1848?

The theories of medicine before 1848 often appeared logical, but prevented further discoveries.

☑ For a long time, many diseases were believed to be caused by supernatural forces. These could only be countered by non-medical treatments.

☑ The Theory of the Four Humours was developed by Hippocrates in Ancient Greece. He believed that illness was caused by an imbalance of four liquids in the body - blood, choler (yellow bile), black bile, and phlegm.

☑ Galen, in the second century BCE, developed Hippocrates' Four Humours Theory with the Theory of Opposites. He suggested that diseases could be cured by providing food and conditions that were opposite to the illness. For example, cold wet food should be eaten by someone with a hot, dry fever.

☑ Miasma, or 'bad air', was believed to cause a lot of illnesses. This belief lasted from medieval times until the nineteenth century.

☑ The spontaneous generation theory suggested that microorganisms were created by decay, and went on to create miasma.

 How did understanding of anatomy help medical progress before 1848?

There were 4 important ways the understanding of anatomy help medical progress before 1848 *(p.34)*.

☑ For hundreds of years, anatomical understanding was based on the work of Galen.

☑ Anatomical discoveries helped doctors to understand the human body and illness better.

☑ In 1543, Andreas Vesalius's book called 'On the Fabric of the Human Body' based on his discoveries in dissection helped doctors to understand the human body better.

☑ In 1628, William Harvey's book 'On the Motion of the Heart and Blood', helped understanding the circulation system.

 What technology helped medicine to progress before 1848?

The development of technology made some medical advances possible.

☑ The introduction of the printing-press to England in 1476 made it easier for doctors and scientists to share ideas.

☑ A growing understanding of iatrochemistry in the 1600s gave doctors new minerals and metals to work with.

☑ The development of water pumps in the 1600s inspired William Harvey to understand the circulation system.

☑ The invention of the microscope in 1665 meant that scientists could see microorganisms.

☑ The invention of the thermometer in 1709 meant that doctors could observe and record body temperature.

THE UNDERSTANDING OF DISEASE IN THE 19TH CENTURY

New ideas gather pace

What was the understanding of disease in the 19th century?

In the mid-nineteenth century, understanding of disease was based on miasma and spontaneous generation.

What did people believe about miasma and disease in the 19th century?

People still believed that disease was carried through bad air.

What was the understanding of spontaneous generation in the 19th century?

Spontaneous generation was a theory that rotting material - such as food and excrement - created microorganisms, which caused miasma and disease.

Why did the understanding of disease not progress in the 19th century?

There were 2 main factors affecting medical progress and understanding in the mid-nineteenth century.

☑ Hospitals relied on charity for funding. There was generally little money available for research.

☑ Doctors wanted to continue to work as they always had, and were reluctant to try new methods for treating patients.

What were the main changes that led to understanding disease in the nineteenth century?

There were 5 main changes that allowed for medical progress in the 19th century.

☑ The development of microscopes allowed Louis Pasteur *(p.40)* to develop and publish his germ theory *(p.40)* in 1861.

☑ Supernatural and religious ideas about disease were dying out.

☑ More hospitals were built, and the work of Florence Nightingale *(p.18)* meant they were a lot cleaner.

☑ The development of anaesthetics and antiseptics led to improvements in surgery.

☑ The government began to take more action and implemented measures to improve public health.

19TH CENTURY HOSPITALS

Better medical knowledge makes an impact

What were hospitals like in the 19th century?

In the early 1800s, hospitals were small organisations that relied on private or charitable funding. However, the pressure to provide medical care resulted in the establishment of general hospitals.

What alternatives to hospitals were available in the nineteenth century?

Hospitals were difficult to get into so alternatives included:

- ☑ A home visit from a doctor who would diagnose the illness and suggest a treatment.
- ☑ The patient's family, or a nurse if they could afford one, would take care of the patient at home. They were expected to ensure that the patient received the treatment, and to keep records of their condition.

How were patients treated in 19th century hospitals?

Hospital patients had to follow rules and behave in a certain way during their stay. Sometimes they were only admitted with a recommendation, written by a doctor or a respected member of the community.

What types of hospitals were there in the 19th century?

There were 3 main types of hospitals in the 19th century.

- ☑ Cottage hospitals, accommodating about 12 patients, were set up from the mid-19th century. They would be run by a local GP.
- ☑ Infirmaries were larger hospitals built in towns and cities. These also provided an outpatient service. Initially they were funded by charities, and were often crowded and dirty.
- ☑ As well as general infirmaries, specialist hospitals were also built, such as the Hospital for Sick Children in Great Ormond Street, which was established in 1852.

DID YOU KNOW?

In the first decades of the Nightingale School For Nurses, trainees were taught by male doctors because there weren't enough trained nurses to teach them.

FLORENCE NIGHTINGALE

The Lady with the Lamp

Who was Florence Nightingale?

Born in 1820, Florence Nightingale became a nurse despite opposition from her family. She cared for patients during the Crimean War, and is often to referred to as the 'Lady with the Lamp'.

What was nursing and hospital care like before Florence Nightingale?

In the early 1800s, most people were cared for by family in their own homes. A doctor would visit the patient and prescribe them medicine. Nurses were untrained and did not keep records on patient care.

Quizzes, amazing exam preparation tools and more at GCSEHistory.com

Why did Nightingale's family not want her to become a nurse?

Prior to Florence Nightingale's influence in the mid-nineteenth century, nursing had a bad reputation, and nurses required no skills or training.

 What did Florence Nightingale do in the Crimean War?

In 1854, during the Crimean War, she went to the Scutari Hospital Barracks in Turkey with a team of 38 nurses, to care for wounded soldiers.

 What problems did Florence Nightingale face upon arrival in the Crimea?

Conditions were terrible for the 10,000 patients, and disease and infection were widespread. Medical supplies were limited, wards were filthy and infested with pests, and the food was poor.

 What were Florence Nightingale's contributions to medicine?

She implemented measures that significantly improved hygiene at Scutari. This included cleaning surfaces, washing bedding, and ensuring the kitchens were clean. The quality of the food given to patients was improved, and windows were opened to allow air to circulate.

 Why did Florence Nightingale make changes at Scutari?

Nightingale believed that miasmas were the cause of illness and that they would be prevented by keeping places clean.

 What impact did Florence Nightingale's actions have at Scutari?

It's believed her actions resulted in the death rate falling from 42% to just 2%. She also became very popular both in the hospital and back in Britain.

 What happened when Florence Nightingale returned from war?

Press coverage of her work in Scutari made Florence Nightingale famous. When she returned to Britain in 1856 she was considered an expert on nursing and hospitals.

 What were Florence Nightingale's achievements?

Florence Nightingale's achievements after she returned from Scutari included writing over 200 books and creating training schools for nurses.

- ☑ In 1859, she wrote the book 'Notes on Nursing', which became a bestseller.
- ☑ The Nightingale Fund was created, which raised over £44,000. She used the money to set up a training school at St Thomas's Hospital in 1860, and a training school for midwives at King's College Hospital in 1861.
- ☑ She played an important role in promoting the French pavilion-design of hospitals, with wider open spaces to prevent miasma, which made them cleaner and safer.

 What impact did Florence Nightingale have on hospitals?

In 'Notes from Nursing', Florence Nightingale set out her ideas about how hospitals were organised.

- ☑ She recommended building hospitals using a design developed in France. The design was based around the pavilion system, to ensure good ventilation through the wards which separated patients, in order to prevent the spread of contagious diseases.
- ☑ She suggested large windows to let in light and air.
- ☑ She also suggested surfaces should be easier to clean, such as tiled floors and painted walls.
- ☑ In 1868, St Thomas' Hospital (where the Nightingale School of Nurses was located) was rebuilt according to Nightingale's recommendations.

What changes did Florence Nightingale bring to nursing?

There were 4 important changes that Florence Nightingale brought to nursing.

- ☑ In 1860, Florence Nightingale opened the Nightingale School For Nurses at St Thomas' Hospital.
- ☑ This introduced strict rules for nurses - they had to go to bed at a certain time, and write a report on their progress every week.
- ☑ It gave nurses a formal training.
- ☑ It raised the status of nursing to a popular profession. By 1900, there were 68,000 trained nurses in Britain.

 Why is Nightingale significant?

Florence Nightingale is regarded the founder of modern nursing. She turned nursing into a respectable profession, and introduced patient care and cleanliness to hospitals.

DID YOU KNOW?

Florence Nightingale did not support the idea of female doctors.

Writing about them in 1860, she said that they 'have only tried to be 'men' and have only succeeded in becoming third-rate men'.

FEMALE DOCTORS

Women fight to become doctors

👤 **Were there many women doctors?**

Women began to train as doctors in the 1800s, although they faced a lot of opposition. Some of the key early female doctors were Elizabeth Garrett-Anderson *(p.21)*, Frances Hoggan, and Sophia Jex-Blake.

⏳ **When were women able to become doctors?**

In 1876, the British government passed a law stating that women should not be prevented from becoming doctors. By 1891, there were 65 female doctors in Britain.

DID YOU KNOW?

The first English woman doctor was Elizabeth Blackwell.

However, she got her medical degree from, and practised in America.

ELIZABETH GARRETT ANDERSON

A pioneering female doctor

Who was Elizabeth Garrett Anderson?

Elizabeth Garrett Anderson was the first woman in Britain to qualify as a doctor. She opened a school of medicine for women, paving the way for women's medical education.

How did Elizabeth Garrett become a doctor?

Garrett Anderson faced opposition as she struggled to become a doctor.

- ☑ She initially trained as a nurse.
- ☑ Her applications were rejected by medical schools, so she trained through private lessons at home.
- ☑ She couldn't apply to the College of Surgeons or the College of Physicians, because their rules said that women were forbidden to do so.
- ☑ She was finally accepted by the Society of Apothecaries in 1865, but only after her father threatened to sue if she wasn't accepted.
- ☑ She then opened St Mary's Dispensary in London, and provided medical treatment for women.
- ☑ She finally gained a medical degree in Paris, after teaching herself French.
- ☑ She became a member of the British Medical Association in 1873. However, both the BMA and the Apothecaries Society changed their regulations after she applied, so that no more women could join.

> **DID YOU KNOW?**
>
> **Apparently, Elizabeth Garrett Anderson dissected corpses in her room at home, as she wasn't allowed in dissecting theatres.**
>
> Elizabeth Garrett Anderson was also the first female mayor in Britain.

FRANCES HOGGAN

A pioneering female doctor and researcher

Who was Frances Hoggan?

Frances Hoggan qualified as a doctor at Zurich University in Switzerland after being refused entry to the Royal Society of Apothecaries.

SOPHIA JEX-BLAKE

A pioneering female doctor

Who was Sophia Jex-Blake?

Sophia Jex-Blake led a group of women to convince Edinburgh University to allow them to study medicine. However, the University refused to allow them to graduate, so she qualified at the University of Bern in Switzerland.

SURGERY

Speed is replaced by anaesthetics, antiseptics and aseptics

What was surgery like in the nineteenth century?

Surgery in the mid-19th century was basic, dangerous, and had a low survival rate.

Why did so many people die in surgery before the late nineteenth century?

Surgery in the mid-19th century had a high mortality rate for 3 main reasons.

- ☑ It was painful, which caused some patients to go into shock and die. It was also hard for them to keep still, and surgeons had to work very fast, which increased the likelihood of mistakes.
- ☑ The wounds created by surgery were likely to become infected.
- ☑ Many patients bled to death.

What pain relief was used for surgery at the beginning of the nineteenth century?

Surgeons used various methods to try and prevent pain in the mid-nineteenth century. These included knocking patients out, giving them alcohol to make them drunk, or giving them opium. None were effective.

What was surgery like in the early nineteenth century?

Patients would usually be held down, and the operation performed as quickly as possible to reduce the amount of pain experienced. Operations often took place in the patient's home.

Why did surgery improve in the late nineteenth century?

The 19th century experienced 4 key changes for surgery.

- ☑ In 1861, Louis Pasteur (p.40) discovered that diseases were caused by germs, paving the way for antiseptic (p.29), and later aseptic, surgery (p.29).
- ☑ Joseph Lister's (p.27) carbolic acid (p.27) spray in 1865 killed germs before and during surgery, reducing infection with antiseptic (p.29) surgery.
- ☑ James Blundell (p.31) carried out early blood transfusions, publishing his paper 'Experiments on the Transfusion of Blood by the Syringe' in 1818.
- ☑ In 1847, James Simpson's (p.26) discovery of chloroform (p.25) reduced pain in surgery, particularly for childbirth.

DID YOU KNOW?

In the 1812 Battle of Borodino, the French surgeon Dominique-Jean Larrey apparently amputated 200 limbs in 24 hours.

ANAESTHETICS

Finding a solution to the problem of pain in surgery

What were anaesthetics?

Anaesthetics were developed during the 1800s to make surgery less painful for the patient.

What types of anaesthetics were used in the nineteenth century?

The use of 3 significant anaesthetics were developed in the nineteenth century:

- ☑ Nitrous oxide *(p.23)*.
- ☑ Ether *(p.24)*.
- ☑ Chloroform *(p.25)*.

DID YOU KNOW?

Humphry Davy discovered the properties of nitrous oxide as a teenaged chemist.

He went on to use it recreationally with friends, and it was thirty years before it was introduced in medicine.

NITROUS OXIDE

Laughing gas

 What was nitrous oxide?

Nitrous oxide, also known as laughing gas *(p.52)*, is an anaesthetic *(p.22)*. It was considered too weak to be suitable for major surgical operations.

 Who discovered nitrous oxide?

Humphry Davy *(p.24)* discovered the anaesthetic *(p.22)* properties of nitrous oxide, although it was American dentist Horace Wells who first used it as an anaesthetic to extract a tooth.

⏳ **When was nitrous oxide first used as an anaesthetic?**

Nitrous oxide was first used as an anaesthetic *(p.22)* in 1844.

DID YOU KNOW?

Horace Wells, an American dentist, suffered a humiliating failure when he tried to demonstrate nitrous oxide as an anaesthetic.

- ✔ The patient cried out during the public tooth extraction at Harvard, so onlookers believed that he had failed. Wells was humiliated, and became addicted to chloroform after self-experimenting.
- ✔ The effects of his addiction caused him to throw acid at two people, and he committed suicide while in prison.

HUMPHRY DAVY

Finding a solution to the problem of pain in surgery

Who was Humphry Davy?

Humphry Davy was a chemist and inventor, who discovered the use of nitrous oxide *(p.23)* as an anaesthetic. *(p.22)*

ETHER

Smelly, sickly and explosive!

What was ether?

Ether was an anaesthetic. *(p.22)*

Why wasn't ether more widely used?

Ether was an effective form of pain relief, but had unpleasant side effects (such as vomiting). It was also highly flammable.

When was ether first successfully used in surgery?

Ether was first used successfully in 1846, in a leg amputation.

Who first used ether successfully?

Robert Liston *(p.24)* first used ether successfully in Britain.

DID YOU KNOW?

American aristocrats were using ether recreationally at the turn of the century.

They would hold parties called 'ether frolics'.

ROBERT LISTON

'The fastest knife on West End'

Who was Robert Liston?

Robert Liston was a surgeon renowned for his speed and strength. He once amputated a leg in 28 seconds. Liston was the first to use ether *(p.24)* as an anaesthetic *(p.22)* during surgery.

CHLOROFORM

'That blessed chloroform!'
Queen Victoria

What is chloroform?

Chloroform was an effective form of pain relief.

Who was the first doctor to use chloroform during surgery?

James Simpson *(p.26)*, a professor of midwifery at Edinburgh University, experimented with chloroform on himself and friends.

When did James Simpson discover that chloroform could be used as an anaesthetic?

James Simpson *(p.26)* discovered that chloroform could be used as an anaesthetic *(p.22)* in 1847.

How did James Simpson first use chloroform?

James Simpson *(p.26)* used chloroform on women in childbirth.

Why was there opposition to the use of chloroform?

There were 3 main reasons why some people opposed the use of chloroform.

- ☑ Some army surgeons believed that soldiers should endure pain.
- ☑ Some religious people believed it was God's intention that women should feel pain in childbirth, and that suffering during surgery was God's will.
- ☑ It was difficult to get the dosage right. This was demonstrated when 14-year-old Hannah Greener died while having an ingrown toenail removed.

Who made chloroform more popular?

Chloroform finally became accepted when Queen Victoria used it during the delivery of her eighth child. After this, patients began to ask for it in their operations.

Why was the use of chloroform dangerous?

Chloroform led to the so-called Black Period of surgery, when death rates increased because, with unconscious patients, surgeons were taking their time and doing more advanced surgeries. This meant they were unknowingly taking infection deeper into the body.

How was chloroform use made safer?

John Snow *(p.35)* developed a type of chloroform inhaler and calculated the correct dose per patient, making it much safer and preventing an overdose.

DID YOU KNOW?

After its discovery, chloroform was sometimes used by criminals in robberies, rapes and murders.

JAMES SIMPSON

The Father of Anaesthetics

Who was James Simpson?

James Simpson was a Scottish doctor in the 1800s who experimented with different types of anaesthetics for use during childbirth. He discovered that chloroform *(p.25)* was effective, and had limited side effects when used in the correct dose.

HANNAH GREENER

14 year old dies of chloroform overdose

Who was Hannah Greener?

Hannah Greener was a 14 year old who died while having surgery, an ingrown toenail removal, in 1848 *(p.34)*. in 1848. It is believed she died of an overdose of chloroform *(p.25)* before dosages were known.

COCAINE AS AN ANAESTHETIC

A new form of pain relief

How was cocaine used in surgery?

Cocaine was used as a local anaesthetic *(p.22)* to numb parts of the body.

When was cocaine used in surgery?

Cocaine was first used as a local anaesthetic *(p.22)* in 1884.

DID YOU KNOW?

In the 19th century, scientists worked out how to extract cocaine from the leaves of the coca tree.

NOVOCAINE AS AN ANAESTHETIC

A new form of pain relief

What was novocaine?

Novocaine was developed in 1903, and was often used as a local anaesthetic. *(p.22)*

👤 Who developed novocaine?

Novocaine was developed by <u>Alford Einhorn</u>, a German chemist. He originally intended it as an anaesthetic *(p.22)* for surgery.

How was novocaine used?

Although Einhorn had originally developed it to use in surgery, novocaine was mostly used in <u>dentistry</u> until the <u>1940s.</u>

What was the significance of novocaine?

Novocaine was a significant development.

- ☑ It was a safer alternative to other local anaesthetics, such as cocaine *(p.26)*.
- ☑ It was one of the first <u>man-made</u> anaesthetics. Its name is taken from 'nova', the Latin for 'new'.

DID YOU KNOW?

Novocaine was originally known as <u>'procaine' when it</u> was first developed.

JOSEPH LISTER
The Father of Aseptic Surgery
and

👤 Who was Joseph Lister?

Joseph Lister was a British surgeon who pioneered the use of antiseptic *(p.29)* techniques in surgery.

CARBOLIC ACID
An effective antiseptic

❓ What was carbolic acid?

Carbolic acid, <u>or phenol,</u> was the first true antiseptic *(p.29)* used in surgery.

⚙ How was carbolic acid discovered?

Joseph Lister *(p.27)* studied Pasteur's *(p.40)* germ theory *(p.40)* and, after realising carbolic acid was effective in stopping wounds from turning gangrenous, he developed a carbolic acid <u>spray to</u> kill germs on both medical instruments and the wound.

⧗ When was carbolic acid first used?

Joseph Lister *(p.27)* first used carbolic acid, in the form of a spray, in <u>1865.</u>

How was carbolic acid used in antiseptic surgery.

Antiseptic *(p.29)* surgery involved cleaning surgical instruments, and the patient's wounds, with carbolic acid.

What results did Lister achieve by using carbolic acid?

By using Lister's *(p.27)* antiseptic *(p.29)* techniques, the death rate among patients who had amputations dropped from 46% to 15%.

 Why was Lister criticised for his use of carbolic acid?

There were 5 main reasons why there was opposition to Lister's *(p.27)* methods.

- ☑ Carbolic acid made the instruments tricky to hold, because they were slippery.
- ☑ Carbolic acid was unpleasant to use, as it irritated surgeons' hands.
- ☑ Doctors applied Lister's *(p.27)* methods incorrectly, leading them to believe his theory was wrong.
- ☑ The equipment was expensive to buy and set up.
- ☑ Lister *(p.27)* was arrogant, and disliked by many of the surgical community.

 Why did Lister use catgut soaked in carbolic acid?

Lister *(p.27)* used catgut as a ligature. It could be soaked in carbolic acid, which helped prevent infection in the wound.

DID YOU KNOW?

Joseph Lister came across the idea of carbolic acid because it was used on fields to neutralise the smell of the sewage used as fertiliser.

He realised that it would be safe to use because it didn't hurt the animals that then grazed on the land.

IGNAZ SEMMELWEIS

Austrian doctor who began to develop aseptic practices

 Who was Ignaz Semmelweis?

Ignaz Semmelweis was a Hungarian doctor who worked at Vienna General Hospital. He recommended that doctors should wash their hands in chloride of lime.

 When was Semmelweis a doctor?

Semmelweis was a doctor during the 1840s.

 How did Semmelweis make his discovery?

Semmelweis realised the death rate among women giving birth in hospital was higher than among those giving birth at home. He believed this was because doctors often delivered babies after dissecting dead bodies.

DID YOU KNOW?

Semmelweis was committed to an insane asylum in 1865, because of his depression.

He was beaten when he tried to leave, and died two weeks later, probably because of blood poisoning from one of the wounds.

ANTISEPTICS
Substances to kill the germs

What are antiseptics?

Antiseptics are subtances used to kill microorganisms and prevent infection.

When were antiseptics developed?

Understanding of infection increased during the 1840s with the work of Ignaz Semmelweis *(p 28)*. The first antiseptic, carbolic acid *(p.27)*, was used by Joseph Lister *(p.27)* in 1865.

ASEPTIC SURGERY
Creating a germ-free environment for surgery

What is aseptic surgery?

Aseptic surgery ensures that operations are carried out in sterile conditions.

What was the difference between antiseptic and aseptic surgery?

Antiseptic *(p.29)* surgery destroys germs on a surgeon's hands, instruments, and immediate surroundings using chemicals e.g. carbolic acid *(p.27)*. Aseptic surgery aims to achieve a completely sterile environment, free from germs, using a combination of measures such as heat and antiseptics.

When was aseptic surgery established?

Aseptic surgery had become common by the year 1900.

What methods were used in aseptic surgery?

There were four key elements to aseptic surgery.

- ☑ Surgeons were scrubbed clean before operating. Today, modern surgeons still 'scrub in' before going into theatre.
- ☑ Surgeons wore new clothes and a fresh pair of thin rubber gloves for each operation.
- ☑ All instruments used during surgery were sterilised beforehand, using steam.
- ☑ The size of operating theatres got smaller, to reduce the risk of infection, and spectators were no longer allowed.

DID YOU KNOW?

Ignaz Semmelweis introduced aseptic procedures in the late 1840s with great success.

The death rate on his Viennese maternity ward fell from 35% to 1% when he instructed his staff to wash their hands with calcium chloride solution.

BLOOD TRANSFUSIONS
Solving the problem of blood-loss

What are blood transfusions?

Blood transfusions are when blood from another person is introduced into a patient's body.

When was the first blood transfusion?

The first blood transfusion was carried out in 1818.

Who discovered blood transfusion?

James Blundell *(p.31)* carried out early blood transfusions, publishing his paper 'Experiments on the Transfusion of Blood by the Syringe' in 1818.

How were blood transfusions performed before the twentieth century?

Because blood clotted when it was removed from the body, early blood transfusions were directly donor-to-patient, and the donor had to be present.

Why were blood transfusions unsuccessful before 1901?

Only 50% of transfusions were successful before 1901.. There were 3 key problems:

- ☑ As blood could not be stored, transfusions involved the donor being directly attached to the recipient by a tube.
- ☑ It could often lead to death through infection.
- ☑ Patients' bodies rejected the new blood because they were given the wrong blood type, as blood groups had yet to be discovered.

How did the discovery of blood groups help in transfusions?

There were 3 key discoveries that led to more successful blood transfusions.

- ☑ In 1901, Karl Landsteiner *(p.31)* discovered the A, B and O blood groups.
- ☑ In 1902, he discovered another blood group, AB.
- ☑ In 1907, it was discovered that type O blood was 'universal' and could safely be given to anyone.

What was the impact of blood transfusions?

Successful and safe blood transfusions helped with medical treatments in 3 main ways.

- ☑ They could be used in surgery.
- ☑ They could help patients suffering from blood disorders such as anaemia or leukaemia.
- ☑ They could be used to help people with liver problems, such as jaundice.

DID YOU KNOW?

In the 17th century, surgeons experimented with blood transfusions between people and sheep.

This had an enormously high death rate, but apparently a few people survived!

Quizzes, amazing exam preparation tools and more at GCSEHistory.com

KARL LANDSTEINER

The Father of Transfusion Medicine

Who was Karl Landsteiner?

Karl Landsteiner was an Austrian scientist who discovered different blood groups, making transfusions safer.

DID YOU KNOW?

Landsteiner received the Nobel Prize in 1930.

JAMES BLUNDELL

First patient to patient blood transfusions doctor

Who is James Blundell?

James Blundell carried out early blood transfusions, publishing his paper 'Experiments on the Transfusion of Blood by the Syringe' in 1818.

PH .

INDUSTRIALISATION

A major change in British society

What was the Industrial Revolution?

Between 1750 and 1900, Britain experienced an industrial revolution, which changed it from a farming society to a nation built on industry.

GOVERNMENT APPROACH

'Let it be'

What was laissez-faire?

Laissez-faire, a French term that translates as 'let it be', was the idea that the government should take a hands-off approach to public health.

DID YOU KNOW?

When cholera first came to Britain in 1831, the government's response was to introduce a national day of prayer and fasting.

PUBLIC HEALTH PROBLEMS

Awful living conditions cause problems to health

What was public health like in the mid-nineteenth century?

Industrialisation had a huge negative impact on public health and living conditions. It led to overcrowding and increased the spread of disease.

How did housing conditions affect public health in industrial Britain?

Houses were built cheaply and as close together as possible. They were usually damp, with little light or ventilation.

How did sanitary conditions affect public health in industrial Britain?

There was usually an inadequate supply of clean water, and poor removal of sewage and rubbish. One toilet could be used by 100 people.

DID YOU KNOW?

Infant mortality was high in industrial towns.

In Manchester in 1842, 57% of all children died before they were five years old.

DISEASE IN INDUSTRIAL BRITAIN

Lice, poor ventilation and dirty water cause ill-health

What diseases were common in the 1800s?

During the nineteenth century, diseases could spread quickly, particularly in towns and cities. The most common were typhoid, cholera *(p.35)*, tuberculosis, and typhus.

Why did disease spread easily in the mid 19th century?

Living conditions in industrial towns and cities were poor, so diseases could spread easily and quickly.

What was typhoid in industrial Britain?

Typhoid was spread via contaminated food and water. Symptoms included headaches and fever.

What was cholera disease in industrial Britain?

Cholera *(p.35)* was spread through contaminated food and water. Symptoms involved extreme vomiting and diarrhoea.

What was tuberculosis in industrial Britain?

Tuberculosis affected the lungs and was spread by infected people sneezing and coughing. It was also more common in badly-ventilated and damp houses. Symptoms included coughing up blood and weight loss.

What was typhus in in the 1850s?

Typhus was spread through body lice. Symptoms included fever and headaches.

EDWIN CHADWICK

A civil servant reports on public health

Who was Edwin Chadwick?

Edwin Chadwick was a civil servant who was involved with the workhouses. He was asked by the government to report on the living conditions and health of the poor.

What was Chadwick's report called?

Chadwick's report, called 'Report on the Sanitary *(p.38)* Conditions of the Labouring Population', was published in 1842.

What conclusions did Chadwick claim in his report?

Edwin Chadwick's report reached 4 main conclusions:

- ✅ Ill-health was caused by the awful conditions in which people lived.
- ✅ If towns were cleaner, there wouldn't be as much disease, and people would not have to take time off work. This would result in fewer people needing the workhouses, which would save ratepayers money.
- ✅ Clean water and sewage disposal was needed for a healthy nation.

Why did Chadwick suggest people could save money by looking after the poor?

Local governments should be responsible for public health and set up boards of health. People would pay taxes to pay for this; but it would save money in the long term, as living conditions improved and fewer people used workhouses.

What did Chadwick recommend to improve health?

Chadwick made two recommendations to address poor living conditions as a cause of disease.

- ✅ A 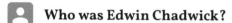drainage system and refuse collections should be organised.
- ✅ A medical officer should be appointed to each area.

How did the government react to Chadwick's proposals?

Chadwick's ideas about increasing rates were not popular. It was not until there was a further cholera *(p.35)* epidemic that the government began to act on his recommendations.

PUBLIC HEALTH ACT, 1848

Encouraging towns to improve public health

What was the Public Health Act of 1848?

The 1848 Public Health Act was the first attempt by the government to enforce the clean up of towns in England and Wales.

What did the Public Health Act 1848 recommend?

The 1848 Public Health Act made four main recommendations.

- ☑ Each town could appoint a Medical Officer of Health.
- ☑ A general Board of Health could be set up, and towns would be allowed to create their own local boards of health.
- ☑ Rubbish removals could be organised, and a sewer system built.
- ☑ People should have access to clean water.

What were the problems with the Public Health Act of 1848?

The Public Health Act had of 1848 had limited impact. There were two main reasons for this.

- ☑ The terms of the Act were only temporary.
- ☑ The Act was voluntary. To create a local board of health required 10% of ratepayers to be in favour, and some local authorities did not take action.

What was the significance of the Public Health Act 1848?

This was the first time the government had passed a law to improve public health, and demonstrates the move away from a laissez-faire *(p.31)* attitude.

Quizzes, amazing exam preparation tools and more at GCSEHistory.com

JOHN SNOW
The Father of Modern Epidemiology

👤 Who was John Snow?
John Snow was the doctor responsible for discovering that cholera *(p.35)* was a water-borne disease.

🔬 What else did John Snow discover?
John Snow also invented an inhaler that could be used to administer chloroform *(p.25)* safely by controlling the dose.

DID YOU KNOW?

John Snow was the doctor responsible for Queen Victoria using chloroform during the birth of her eighth child.

After this, Victoria referred to it as 'that blessed chloroform!'. This contributed to the public acceptance of the use of the anaesthetic.

CHOLERA
The 'Blue Death'

❓ What is cholera?
Cholera is a potentially deadly disease that causes severe sickness, diarrhoea and dehydration.

🔬 What was cholera's nickname?
Cholera was nicknamed 'the blue death' as it ruptured blood vessels, and skin turned blue as people became dehydrated.

🔬 When were there outbreaks of cholera?
Cholera first arrived in Britain in 1831. There were further outbreaks in 1848 *(p.34)*, 1853, and 1865.

🔬 How many people died in each outbreak of cholera?
The number of deaths varied in each outbreak:
- ☑ In 1831-32, London suffered 5,275 deaths. In total, the outbreak killed 21,882 across Britain.
- ☑ In 1848 *(p.34)*-49, 53,292 people died.
- ☑ In 1853-54, 20,097 people died.
- ☑ In 1865-66, 14,378 people died.

👤 Who discovered the causes for cholera?
A doctor called John Snow *(p.35)*.

🔬 How did John Snow discover the cause of cholera?
Snow *(p.35)* studied deaths from cholera and made a map of them. He traced the source of the outbreak to a water pump on Broad Street, London.

When was the cause of cholera discovered?

The cause of cholera was discovered in 1854.

 What did John Snow think about the causes of cholera?

As many of the victims of the 1854 outbreak lived near a water pump on Broad Street, Snow *(p.35)* theorised that cholera could not be caused by miasma and was instead spread by contaminated water.

 What was done to prevent the spread of cholera?

The government had a laissez-faire *(p.31)* attitude, which meant that they stayed out of public health issues. As a result, people tried 2 main ways to prevent cholera:

✅ Many thought it was caused by miasma, so tried to prevent it by cleaning up dirty streets.

✅ In 1848 *(p.34)*, the first Public Health Act suggested that towns and cities provide clean water supplies. However, as it was not compulsory, its impact was limited.

 Why was there opposition to John Snow's discovery of the cause of cholera?

Some doctors disagreed with Snow's *(p.35)* findings. Pasteur's *(p.40)* germ theory *(p.40)* had not been published so Snow's idea that cholera was transmitted through contaminated water, rather than through miasma could not be proven.

 How was the cholera outbreak of 1854 ended?

Snow *(p.35)* asked for the handle of the Broad Street water pump to be removed, so people could not use it. The outbreak quickly ended, proving the disease had come from the water in the pump. It was later found that a cesspit had been leaking into the well.

 Why were Snow's cholera findings important?

John Snow *(p.35)* had 2 main impacts.

✅ In 1855, he presented the results of his investigation to Parliament, and suggested that a new sewer system was built, something the government later agreed to.

✅ Snow *(p.35)* proved that cholera was not carried through the air like a poisonous gas *(p.52)* or miasma.

DID YOU KNOW?

A cholera victim could expel up to 20 litres of diarrhoea.

GREAT STINK, 1858

The filthy River Thames becomes impossible to ignore

 What was the Great Stink?

A heatwave in the summer of 1858 caused the River Thames to smell much worse than it usually did, due to the evaporation of water. As a result, the river had a more concentrated sewage content.

How did Parliament react to the Great Stink?

The smell was so bad that politicians in the Houses of Parliament, next to the river, demanded to meet somewhere else. MPs asked for help from Joseph Bazalgette *(p.37)*, a civil engineer.

What was the significance of the Great Stink?

The Great Stink of 1858 had 2 main effects.

☑ The sewer system beneath London was built, which greatly improved conditions in the city.

☑ The Great Stink marked the end of the laissez-faire *(p.31)* attitude of government.

DID YOU KNOW?

Temperatures during the summer of 1858 reached over 30 degrees celsius.

JOSEPH BAZALGETTE

Master engineer builds the London sewers

Who was Joseph Bazalgette?

Joseph Bazalgette was a civil engineer in the 1800s.

What was Bazalgette's contribution to public health?

He was the chief designer and engineer on London's sewer system, ordered after the Great Stink *(p.36)*.

What was Bazalgette's sewer system like?

It was designed to remove waste from London's streets by carrying waste downriver towards the sea. The main sewers covered a distance of 83 miles and removed 420 million gallons of sewage per day.

When was Bazalgette's sewer system built?

The system was offically opened in 1865, although the system continued to be developed into the 1870s.

How much did Bazalgette's sewer system cost?

The system cost £3 million.

DID YOU KNOW?

Bazalgette's sewers used 318 million bricks!

There were a total of about 1,300 miles of sewer built under London, and the project took 7 years.

SANITARY ACT, 1866

Appointing inspectors

❓ What was the Sanitary Act of 1866?

The Sanitary Act of 1866 required towns to appoint <u>inspectors</u> to check on <u>water supplies</u> and <u>drainage.</u>

PUBLIC HEALTH ACT, 1875

Forcing towns to improve public health

❓ What was the Public Health Act of 1875?

The second Public Health Act of 1875 was the government's attempt to enforce action to reduce some public health-related illnesses and diseases, such as cholera *(p.35)*.

Why did the government pass the Public Health Act 1875?

The second Public Health Act of 1875 was passed as the government began to realise that public health was part of their responsibility.

What measures were in the 1875 Public Health Act?

The Public Health Act of 1875 made local authorities responsible for 3 main areas of public health measures.

- ☑ There must be provision of clean <u>water</u> and proper disposal of <u>rubbish and sewage.</u>
- ☑ <u>Medical Officers</u> of Health should be appointed in every area.
- ☑ There were standards for new <u>housing, and</u> lodging houses should be checked.

Why was the 1875 Public Health Act an improvement on the 1848 Public Health Act?

The 1875 Health Act was different from the 1848 *(p.34)* Health Act because it was compulsory - local authorities were forced to carry out the improvements.

Why was the 1875 Public Health Act significant?

The second act signified a change in the government's laissez-faire *(p.31)* attitude. Laws were now being passed to improve public health and they had to be obeyed.

DID YOU KNOW?

In 1867 Manchester led the country in toilets.

The local authorities abolished midden privies (a toilet over a pit) and replaced them with pail privies. These were much easier to empty and clean.

Quizzes, amazing exam preparation tools and more at GCSEHistory.com

LIBERAL REFORMS

The Liberal government of 1906 introduces many reforms that improve health

What was the purpose of the Liberal reforms from 1906?

After the Liberal Party won the 1906 general election by a landslide, they began to introduce reforms to tackle poverty. Poverty was the cause of many health problems in British society.

Who did the Liberal reforms try to help?

The Liberal reforms aimed to help the most vulnerable members of society:

- ☑ The young.
- ☑ The old.
- ☑ The sick.
- ☑ The unemployed.

Why did the Liberal Party introduce reforms after 1906?

By 1906, there were 4 main factors which contributed to people realising that poverty was a very real problem in Britain:

- ☑ Social studies by Rowntree *(p.40)* and Booth *(p.40)* between 1891 and 1903, showed that many people lived below the poverty line, suffering from malnutrition and poor health.
- ☑ Britain needed a strong, healthy army to defend its empire. However, more than a third of recruits for the Boer War (1899-1902) were unfit as a result of poverty.
- ☑ People had to pay to see a doctor. Some doctors had 'sick clubs', where people paid an amount each week to cover their costs, but many people couldn't afford medical care.
- ☑ The Industrial Revolution *(p.31)* had reduced the health of the people as it had created poor living conditions for the working classes. This had increased disease.

How did the Liberal reforms help children?

The Liberals introduced 3 main laws, between 1906 and 1908, to reduce poverty and ill-health in children:

- ☑ The Free School Meals Act of 1906 allowed local authorities to provide free school meals from local taxes, although many chose not to.
- ☑ In 1907, free medical inspections were introduced in schools.
- ☑ In 1908, the Children's Act made it illegal to neglect children, or to sell them alcohol or tobacco.

How did the Liberal reforms help the elderly?

In 1908, an 'old age pension' of five shillings a week was introduced for poor people over the age of 70.

How did the Liberal reforms help the unemployed?

In 1909, Labour Exchanges were developed to help the unemployed look for work. In 1911, the National Insurance Act provided them with unemployment payments.

How did the National Insurance Act, introduced under the Liberal reforms, help workers?

The National Insurance Act of 1911 provided a number of benefits to workers:

- ☑ It provided sick pay to ill workers, and allowed them to access free medical treatment.
- ☑ It paid money to workers without jobs for up to 15 weeks, and prevented them falling into poverty.
- ☑ It was paid for by contributions from employers, the government, and the workers themselves.

SEEBOHM ROWNTREE

Victorian Quaker and philanthropist

Who is Seebohm Rowntree?

Seebohm Rowntree was a Victorian philanthropist, who fought for social justice in line with his Quaker beliefs. His report was called 'Poverty, a Study of Town Life'.

CHARLES BOOTH

Victorian philanthropist

Who is Charles Booth?

Charles Booth was a Victorian philanthropist who fought for social justice. He published several surveys he had undertaken, in 'Life and Labour of the People'.

LOUIS PASTEUR

'Chance only favours prepared minds'
Louis Pasteur

Who was Louis Pasteur?

Louis Pasteur was a French scientist who discovered germs and proved a direct connection between germs and disease.

When was Pasteur's germ theory published?

Louis Pasteur published his work on germ theory in 1861. In 1878, he published the next stage of his theory - that germs caused infection.

What was Pasteur's germ theory?

This was the theory that germs caused disease. It disproved previous beliefs about other causes, such as miasma.

What are the principles Pasteur's theory?

There were four basic principles of germ theory.

☑ The air contains living microorganisms.

Quizzes, amazing exam preparation tools and more at GCSEHistory.com

Microbes in the air cause decay.

Microbes are not evenly distributed in the air.

Microbes can be killed by heating them.

What led to Pasteur's germ theory?

In 1857, Pasteur was employed by a French brewery to work out why their beer kept going sour.

How did Pasteur make his discovery?

Using a microscope, he discovered microorganisms growing in the liquid. He realised that sterilising water, and keeping it in a sealed flask, prevented microorganisms from entering it. If the sterilised water was kept in an open flask, the microbes would breed again.

What was Pasteur's process of 'pasteurisation'?

Pasteur called the process of heating liquid to kill bacteria 'pasteurisation'.

How did Pasteur make the link between germs and disease?

In 1865, Pasteur was asked to investigate a problem in the silk industry. He discovered that silkworms were dying from microorganisms and subsequently made the link between germs and disease.

Why did doctors oppose Pasteur's theory?

Because microorganisms could be seen everywhere, for example in human blood, doctors could not understand why some caused disease and others did not.

What was the impact of Pasteur's germ theory?

There were 4 main results of germ theory.

✅ It demonstrated the belief that disease was created by spontaneous generation was wrong. However, spontaneous generation was still an influential idea that some doctors, such as Dr Henry Bastian, still supported.

✅ Between 1876 and 1883, Robert Koch *(p.42)* discovered that different bacteria cause different diseases.

✅ It led to an understanding of why infection occurred in surgery.

✅ It led to Lister's *(p.27)* use of carbolic acid *(p.27)* as an antiseptic *(p.29)* in surgery.

How did Pasteur discover a vaccine for chicken cholera?

The chicken cholera *(p.35)* vaccine was discovered by chance in 1879. A mistake by Pasteur's assistant led to the realisation that the germ was weakened when exposed to air. Injecting the weakened germ into chickens stopped them from catching the disease.

How did Pasteur help the development of vaccines?

Pasteur helped discover two other vaccines.

✅ In 1881, Pasteur's team produced a weakened strain of anthrax that would prevent the disease in sheep.

✅ In 1885, Pasteur successfully cured a boy from rabies by using a vaccine for the disease he had developed.

How did Pasteur's rivalry with Koch lead to scientific breakthroughs?

There are 5 main reasons why the rivalry between Pasteur and Koch *(p.42)* led to scientific breakthroughs.

✅ Both were researching during the Franco-Prussian War, and defeating diseases could have a big impact on the battlefield.

- ☑ The governments of France and Germany paid for the laboratories and teams of scientists, for Pasteur and Koch *(p.42)* respectively.
- ☑ The individual characters of both men played a role. Both were relentless in their attempts to make scientific advances. For Pasteur, this resulted in his scientific breakthrough about germ theory; and for Koch *(p.42)* it resulted in his discoveries about tuberculosis (TB) and cholera *(p.35)*.
- ☑ Communication increased the rivalry, as Koch *(p.42)* heard about Pasteur's discoveries quickly, helping him to make breakthroughs of his own.
- ☑ Teamwork and rivalry contributed to breakthroughs, as both sides quickly wanted to discover vaccinations for contagious diseases such as diphtheria.

> ### DID YOU KNOW?
> Three of Louis Pasteur's five children died of typhoid.

ROBERT KOCH
Taking germ theory to the next level

Who was Robert Koch?

Robert Koch was a German doctor considered to be the founder of modern bacteriology.

What were Koch's achievements?

Koch's work was important for 3 main reasons.

- ☑ He developed a method for staining and photographing microorganisms using dye.
- ☑ He discovered the specific germs that caused a number of diseases: anthrax in 1876, tuberculosis in 1882, and cholera *(p.35)* in 1883.
- ☑ He developed the use of agar jelly for growing bacterial cultures on which he could experiment.
- ☑ He developed a steam steriliser which used heat to sterilise equipment and dressings.

How did Koch prove that cholera was spread through contaminated water?

In 1884, he found cholera *(p.35)* in drinking water in Calcutta, India, which proved it was spread in water supplies. This confirmed John Snow's *(p.35)* theory of why cholera had spread in London in 1854.

What was the significance of Koch's work?

Koch's work was a major breakthrough and he had 2 key impacts on medicine.

- ☑ Doctors began to study disease itself, rather than studying and treating symptoms.
- ☑ He made it easier for other scientists to identify and study bacteria, such as diphtheria and pneumonia, because of his staining technique.

Why were Koch and Pasteur rivals?

Koch and Pasteur *(p.40)* were rivals for two key reasons:

- ☑ They fell out at an 1882 conference over a mistranslated term in Pasteur's *(p.40)* lecture. Two of Koch's students then wrote a long paper criticising Pasteur's findings on anthrax.

✅ Their countries were at war between 1870-71, and their respective governments gave them funding for research and equipment.

DID YOU KNOW?

Koch was a childhood prodigy
He taught himself to read newspapers when he was only 5, he loved to read the classics, and also became an expert in chess.

EMIL VON BEHRING

Discovering anti-toxins to treat diphtheria

Who was Emil von Behring?

Emil von Behring was the scientist who discovered that antitoxins could be used to successfully treat diphtheria.

When did Emil von Behring discover antitoxins?

Emil von Behring discovered antitoxins in 1890.

DID YOU KNOW?

Emil von Behring was awarded the Nobel Prize in 1901

ANTITOXINS

Another treatment for disease

What are antitoxins?

Antitoxins are produced by the body's white blood cells and can be used to prevent germs from producing poisons.

X-RAYS IN THE FIRST WORLD WAR

A way to see inside the body

How do x-rays work?

X-rays work by passing radiation *(p.44)* through the body to produce images of bones, organs and tissue.

Who invented the X-ray machine?

The X-ray machine was invented by a German physicist named Wilhelm Roentgen *(p.44)*.

⧗ When was the X-ray machine invented?

The X-ray machine was invented in 1895. The X-ray machine was very quickly put to use and was being used in London hospitals by 1896.

🔬 How could X-rays assist in medical treatment?

X-ray machines helped doctors in 4 key ways:

- ☑ They could show <u>broken bones so</u> they could be set properly.
- ☑ They could show where <u>bullets or o</u>ther foreign objects were lodged in the body.
- ☑ They could be used to identify the shadow on a lung that indicated tuberculosis.
- ☑ They could be used to show internal organs if the patient swallowed something that showed up on the X-ray.

> **DID YOU KNOW?**
>
> ---
>
> **Doctors were quick to obtain and experiment with X-ray machines.**
>
> John MacIntyre, at Glasgow Royal Infirmary, produced X-rays of a penny in a child's throat and a frog kicking its legs.

WILHELM ROENTGEN

The scientist who discovered x-rays

👤 Who was Wilhelm Roentgen?

Wilhelm Roentgen was a German physicist, who first discovered that radiation *(p.44)* could be used to produce an image of bones inside the body. He invented a machine that became known as the X-ray *(p.43)* machine.

RADIATION

Used as a treatment for cancer

❓ What is radiation?

Radiation is the emission or transmission of energy through space or through material, which takes place in the form of waves or particles. These particles can be used to treat certain diseases and illnesses.

MARIE CURIE

Scientist who investigated radiation.

Who was Marie Curie?

Marie Curie was a Polish chemist who was awarded a Nobel Prize in 1903. She worked on radioactive elements, and died of radiation *(p.44)* exposure.

What discoveries did Marie Curie make?

Marie Curie made 2 important discoveries.

- ☑ She found two new radioactive elements, polonium and radium, in 1898.
- ☑ She discovered that radiation *(p.44)* could be used to shrink tumours.

What did Marie Curie do in the First World War?

Marie Curie was involved in 2 main activities during the First World War *(p.51)*:

- ☑ She put her research into a bank, and spent the First World War *(p.51)* building mobile X-rays in cars and portable X-rays for base hospitals.
- ☑ She trained over 150 female friends and volunteers on how to drive and use the X-rays. They then drove these radiological cars, known as 'little Curies', around the Western Front to help the war effort.

DID YOU KNOW?

During the First World War, Marie Curie donated twenty mobile X-ray units to the French army.

These were known as 'petite Curies' (little Curies).

MAGIC BULLET

Targetting the germs that cause disease

What is a magic bullet?

A magic bullet is a chemical compound that will kill a specific germ without harming other cells.

Who discovered the magic bullet?

Paul Ehrlich *(p.46)* worked with Robert Koch *(p.42)*, Emil von Behring *(p.43)* and Sahachiro Hata *(p.46)*. He is known for discovering the first 'magic bullet'.

How did Paul Ehrlich discover the first magic bullet?

There were 2 main stages in Ehrlich's *(p.46)* discovery of magic bullets.

- ☑ In 1900, he suggested some chemicals might be able to kill specific germs.
- ☑ In 1909, Paul Ehrlich *(p.46)* and Sahachiro Hata *(p.46)* discovered the compound Salvarsan 606, which could kill the syphilis germ.

What was the first magic bullet?

The first magic bullet was Salvarsan 606, which was the 606th chemical compound tested by Ehrlich's *(p.46)* team to treat syphilis.

What was the impact of the discovery of magic bullets?

Magic bullets had 3 key impacts on medicine.

- ☑ The discovery of magic bullets marked the birth of the modern pharmaceutical industry.
- ☑ In 1932, Gerhard Domagk *(p.48)* discovered that blood poisoning could be cured using Prontosil *(p.47)*.
- ☑ In 1935, French and Italian scientists at the Pasteur *(p.40)* Institute in Paris discovered bacteriostatic antibiotics based on how Prontosil *(p.47)* affected the body. They had realised that bacteria in the body could not multiply because of Prontosil.

When were magic bullets developed?

The development of magic bullets took a number of years.

- ☑ The idea of magic bullets was first suggested by Paul Ehrlich *(p.46)* in 1900.
- ☑ Salvarsan 606, the first magic bullet, was discovered in 1909.

DID YOU KNOW?

As well as discovering the cure for syphilis, Paul Ehrlich made a number of other significant medical discoveries.

He also made medical breakthroughs in haematology, chemotherapy, and immunology.

PAUL EHRLICH

The doctor who discovered Prontosil

Who was Paul Ehrlich?

Paul Ehrlich was German scientist and physician. He studied blood and immunology, and discovered the cure for syphilis, Salvarsan 606. He was awarded a Nobel Prize in 1908.

SAHACHIRO HATA

Part of the team who discovered the magic bullet

Who was Sahachiro Hata?

Sahachiro Hata is known for being part of the team that discovered the first 'magic bullet *(p.45)*'.

PRONTOSIL

A red dye becomes a cure

What was Prontosil?

Prontosil is a chemical used to make a red dye that contains <u>sulphonamide. It</u> was found to be the 'magic bullet *(p.45)*' that killed the streptococcus infection.

When was Prontosil discovered?

Gerhard Domagk *(p.48)* discovered Prontosil could kill <u>streptococcus</u> in <u>1932.</u>

How did Domagk test Prontosil?

In 1935, Gerhard Domagk *(p.48)* used Prontosil to cure his daughter of infection.

Who discovered Prontosil?

Gerhard Domagk *(p.48)* was a German scientist who discovered that Prontosil could be used as a magic bullet *(p.45)* against bacteria that caused infection.

What was Prontosil used for?

The discovery of Prontosil's magic bullet *(p.45)* properties was useful in 2 main ways.

- ☑ It was found to be effective in curing <u>puerperal fever in</u> new mothers.
- ☑ The main ingredient, sulphonamide, was developed to treat <u>pneumonia, scarlet fever and meningitis.</u>

GERHARD DOMAGK

German pathologist and bacteriologist

Who was Gerhard Domagk?

Gerhard Domagk was a German scientist who discovered that Prontosil *(p.47)* could be used as a magic bullet *(p.45)* against bacteria that caused infection.

ALEXANDER FLEMING

Discovering penicillin

Who was Alexander Fleming?

Sir Alexander Fleming was a Scottish scientist, who discovered the antibiotic *(p.49)* properties of penicillin in 1928.

What was Alexander Fleming's background?

Alexander Fleming had been an army doctor *(p.64)* in the First World War *(p.51)*, where he saw many men die of infection caused by the staphylococcus bacteria and septicaemia.

What were Fleming's early discoveries?

In 1922, Fleming's research identified that an enzyme called lysozyme, found in human tears, killed certain harmless bacteria.

How did Fleming discover penicillin?

In 1928, Fleming accidentally left some staphylococcus bacteria on a culture plate in his lab. After two weeks he noticed that penicillium notatum (a green *(p.26)* mould) had stopped the bacteria from growing.

Where did Fleming publish his findings?

In 1929, Fleming published his findings about penicillin *(p.49)* in the 'British Journal of Experimental Pathology'.

What problems did Fleming face?

Fleming was unable to develop his research into penicillin *(p.49)* after 1929 for 3 key reasons:

- ☑ It was difficult to grow enough penicillium (the fungus) for effective research.
- ☑ Penicillin *(p.49)* appeared to take time to have an effect, and its effectiveness was limited when mixed with blood.
- ☑ Fleming was unable to get funding for more research.

DID YOU KNOW?

Fleming studied a wide range of sciences.

He was a biologist, physician, microbiologist, and pharmacologist.

PENICILLIN
Developing the use of antibiotics

What is penicillin?
Penicillin was the first antibiotic to be discovered, and was originally derived from common penicillium mould.

What type of medicine is penicillin?
Antibiotics are microbes that can kill the germs that cause diseases.

How did people use penicillin before it was discovered?
In the Middle Ages, people used mouldy bread to treat infection in a wound, and in 1871 Joseph Lister *(p.27)* used it to treat a patient.

When was penicillin discovered?
Penicillin was discovered in 1928.

What bacteria did penicillin treat?
The staphylococcus bacteria is a germ that causes many infections.

Who developed Fleming's research on penicillin?
In 1939, Howard Florey *(p.50)* and Ernst Chain *(p.50)* at Oxford University began to look into Fleming's *(p.48)* discoveries. Helped by Norman Heatley *(p.51)*, they conducted more tests.

How did Florey and Chain test penicillin?
Florey *(p.50)* and Chain *(p.50)* tested penicillin in 3 stages although they found it difficult to produce enough to be effective:

- ☑ In 1940, their first tests were on mice, which recovered from streptococci with penicillin.
- ☑ In 1941, their first human subject was a policeman with septicaemia. The penicillin helped, but there was not enough to cure him and he died.
- ☑ They developed penicillin to treat children, as a smaller dose was needed.

Who funded the development of penicillin?
Americans were initially responsible for funding the large-scale production of penicillin. Florey *(p.50)* travelled to the U.S. to seek help from the American pharmaceutical industry. They convinced four drug companies to invest.

Why was it possible to mass-produce penicillin?
Penicillin could be mass-produced for 5 key reasons:

- ☑ Individuals such as Fleming *(p.48)*, Florey *(p.50)* and Chain *(p.50)* were actively looking for solutions to infections. Florey's decision not to patent their findings made penicillin affordable.
- ☑ The development of techniques to grow and observe germs helped scientists discover antibiotics.
- ☑ The First World War *(p.51)* showed the impact that infections could have in wartime, while the Second World War gave governments the incentive to find and fund solutions.
- ☑ The technological advance of mass production techniques made it easier to make penicillin.
- ☑ The American government funded Florey's *(p.50)* research for five years. Institutions such as governments funded and encouraged the production of penicillin.

What is the impact of penicillin?

Penicillin is estimated to have saved 200 million lives since its development.

 How has penicillin been developed further?

A synthetic (chemical) version of penicillin was created in 1955.

 Who got the Nobel Prize for penicillin?

In 1945, Fleming *(p.48)*, Florey *(p.50)* and Chain *(p.50)* were jointly awarded the Nobel Prize for Medicine for their work on penicillin.

 Why are scientists constantly researching new antibiotics?

Scientists are constantly working on researching and finding new antibiotics. This is because of the problem of the development of penicillin-resistant bacteria.

DID YOU KNOW?

In the early stages of their research, Florey and Chain struggled to grow enough penicillin to treat a human.

Because there was so little penicillin in the mould, they grew mould on as many available surfaces as they could - including milk bottles, tea trays and bedpans. Later, Americans would use gigantic beer vats to produce the mould.

HOWARD FLOREY

Australian pathologist who developed research into penicillin

 Who was Howard Florey?

Howard Florey was an Australian scientist who worked with Ernst Chain *(p.50)* to further research the potential of penicillin *(p.49)*.

ERNST CHAIN

German biochemist who developed research into penicillin

 Who was Ernst Chain?

Ernst Chain was a German scientist who worked with Howard Florey *(p.50)* to develop tests on penicillin *(p.49)*.

NORMAN HEATLEY

On the team with Florey and Chain

Who was Heatley

Norman Heatley was a biochemist, who helped Howard Florey *(p.50)* and Ernst Chain *(p.50)* develop equipment to test penicillin *(p.49)*.

THE FIRST WORLD WAR CONTEXT

A new sort of warfare... and new medical challenges

How was the First World War fought?

By the end of 1914, both the Allied and German forces had stopped advancing. In order to try to hold the territory they had, each side dug trenches. A new type of warfare had begun.

Which First World War battles were important for medical treatment?

There were many significant locations, events and battles in the First World War. However, some of the most important in the development of medical treatment were:

- ☑ First Battle of Ypres.
- ☑ Hill 60.
- ☑ Second Battle of Ypres.
- ☑ The Somme.
- ☑ Third Battle of Ypres.
- ☑ Arras.
- ☑ Cambrai.

DID YOU KNOW?

The First World War caused 20 million deaths worldwide, and an estimated 21 million injuries.

THE FIRST WORLD WAR TRENCH SYSTEM

Terrible living and fighting conditions on the Western Front

What was the trench system?

Both sides dug networks of trenches to hold their positions on the Western Front. As they were developed they became more sophisticated, and became the soldiers' homes as well as where they fought.

What were the key features of the trench system?

The trenches had 7 key features.

✅ Frontline trench. This was the first line of defence, and soldiers attacked from here.

✅ Support trench. This had support troops, and was also a place to retreat to if the front line was attacked and over-run.

✅ Reserve trench. This was sited 100m behind the support trench. Troops could rest here when they were not on the front line.

✅ Dugouts. These were holes, dug into the sides of trenches, where men could sleep or take cover.

✅ Communication trenches. These were used to connect the other trenches together.

✅ Trenches were cut in a zigzag pattern to stop bullets travelling a long way down them during an attack, or to stop explosions from travelling along the whole trench.

✅ No man's land. This was the space between the front lines of each side's trenches.

DID YOU KNOW?

Soldiers were rotated from the front-line, to the reserve trenches, to rest camps.

Typically, they would spend eight days in the front-line, four in the reserve trenches, and four in the rest camps or nearby towns.

THE USE OF GAS IN THE FIRST WORLD WAR

Chlorine, Phosgene, Mustard

(?) **What were the effects of poison gas in the First World War?**

The use of different types of poison gas caused respiratory problems, blindness and chemical burns.

What types of gas were used in the First World War?

There were 3 main types of gas used for attacks in the First World War *(p.51)*.

✅ Chlorine, which caused death by suffocation.

✅ Phosgene, which led to death by suffocation but acted faster than chlorine.

✅ Mustard gas, which was odourless and caused more than 80% of gas injuries to British soldiers. It <u>burned</u> their skin, eyes and lungs. Mustard gas wasn't introduced until <u>1917.</u>

What effect did gas masks have?

Soldiers were given gas masks, from <u>July 1915,</u> to prevent them inhaling gas, but sometimes they did not get them on quickly enough.

DID YOU KNOW?

Chlorine gas was described as having a smell like a mix of pepper and pineapple.

FIRST WORLD WAR WEAPONS

New weapons made this a terrible war

What new injuries were caused by the new weapons in the First World War?

The rapid developments in military technology meant medical staff had to learn to treat new injuries caused by the new weaponry. These included shrapnel and large explosive wounds, head injuries, gas *(p.52)*, and shell shock *(p.54)*.

What sort of injuries were caused by First World War weapons?

The use of new weapons caused new types of injury in the First World War *(p.51)*.

- ☑ Bullets from rifles and machine guns, as well as sharp pieces of metal (shrapnel), could become deeply embedded in the body.
- ☑ Flying metal from explosive shells, called shrapnel, fired by heavy artillery, could cause large, tearing wounds.
- ☑ Bullets could break bones, which then stuck out through the skin. This was called a compound fracture.
- ☑ There was a huge increase in head injuries from explosions and bullets.
- ☑ Poison gas could cause respiratory problems, blindness, and burns.

DID YOU KNOW?

Studies suggest that only 5.6% of injured soldiers died after receiving medical treatment on the Western Front.

Of the 2.7 million British casualties, 700,000 died before they could receive medical treatment.

THE PROBLEM OF MUD IN THE FIRST WORLD WAR

Problems of hygiene and infection

What was the effect of mud on the Western Front?

Much of the Western Front lay on farmland, which became very muddy in rain. The mud also contained manure and fertilisers. Soldiers had to stand and live in wet, muddy conditions for long periods of time.

What problems did mud cause to medical staff in the First World War?

The mud caused 3 main problems for the medical staff:

- ☑ Trench foot *(p.55)* was a condition caused by prolonged exposure to the damp and cold. Soldiers' feet were frequently soaked and immersed in mud and water, and could not be dried. The skin rotted, which was incredibly painful, and sometimes led to amputation.
- ☑ Mud could enter soldiers' bodies and wounds along with bullets or shrapnel, causing infection.
- ☑ Explosives churned up the land. Many soldiers were drowned and lost in the deep churned mud.

DID YOU KNOW?

The mud on the Western Front was more likely to cause infection because it was farmland.

Before the war, the use of fertilisers meant that there were more bacteria in the earth.

ILLNESSES IN THE FIRST WORLD WAR

Terrible living conditions cause ill-health

How did people get ill in the First World War trenches?

Living and fighting in the trenches caused soldiers to suffer from a number of illnesses, mainly just from the awful conditions in the trenches.

Why did the trenches make people ill?

The poor conditions, and persistent stress of living in the trenches, led to a number of physical and psychological illnesses.

What common illnesses during the First World War were caused by life in the trenches?

Life in the trenches caused many illnesses, but 5 of the most important were:

- ☑ Shell shock *(p.54)*.
- ☑ Trench foot *(p.55)*.
- ☑ Trench fever *(p.56)*.
- ☑ Dysentery *(p.56)*.
- ☑ Gangrene. *(p.56)*

DID YOU KNOW?

About 60% of soldiers are estimated to have suffered from trench fever at some stage during the war.

SHELL SHOCK

Breakdowns caused by the stress of war.

What was shell shock?

The stress of living and fighting in the trenches often caused psychological and mental health problems, known as 'shell shock'.

What were the symptoms of shell shock?

Shell shock could cause nightmares, loss of speech, uncontrollable shaking, and total mental breakdown.

What was the treatment for shell shock?

There was not much understanding about shell shock during the First World War *(p.51)*. It was often seen as hysteria, or an attempt to get out of the war.

- ☑ Some men who suffered from shell shock were accused of cowardice, and punished.
- ☑ Attitudes towards those who suffered from shell shock could be harsh, and they were often accused of cowardice and malingering.
- ☑ Electric shock treatments were sometimes used.
- ☑ Many shell shock patients were cared for at home or sent to mental asylums.
- ☑ 2,000 men were treated for shell shock, including the poets Siegfried Sassoon and Wilfred Owen, at Craiglockhart Hospital in Scotland.

DID YOU KNOW?

Over the course of the First World War, 306 British troops were executed by the army.

They were found guilty of crimes such as desertion and cowardice. It is highly likely that some of them were suffering from shell shock.

TRENCH FOOT

Waterlogged feet become infected

What was trench foot?

Standing in cold, wet water led to a condition called trench foot, where the skin was soaked for such long periods of time that it began to rot. It was extremely painful and sometimes led to amputation of the foot.

How was trench foot prevented?

By 1915, the army understood that persistently cold, wet feet led to trench foot. Officials introduced several ways to try and prevent this.

- ☑ The feet were rubbed with whale oil to protect them.
- ☑ There were regular foot inspections by officers.
- ☑ Soldiers were instructed to change into clean, dry socks.

DID YOU KNOW?

Between 1914 and 1915, an estimated 20,000 British soldiers were treated for trench foot.

TRENCH FEVER

Flu-like symptoms, caused by lice

❓ What was trench fever?

Trench fever affected up to half a million men, causing headaches, high temperatures, and flu-like symptoms.

🔬 What caused trench fever?

Rats and lice carried disease through the trenches.

🔬 How was trench fever prevented in the First World War?

By 1918, it was discovered that one way trench fever was spread was by lice; this led to the introduction of delousing stations.

DID YOU KNOW?

Trench fever could cause temperatures of 40.5 degrees celsius, that lasted for five to six days.

DYSENTERY

Stomach pains and severe diarrhoea

❓ What caused dysentery in the First World War?

Dysentery spread because of the unhygienic latrines and lack of clean water in the trenches. It caused stomach pains, high temperature, diarrhoea, and even death from dehydration.

🔬 How was dysentery prevented in the First World War?

The army began to purify water by adding chloride of lime, but many soldiers didn't like the taste.

DID YOU KNOW?

Latrines in the trenches were a common target for snipers.

GANGRENE

Infections that caused the body tissue to rot

❓ What caused gangrene in the First World War?

Gangrene is the death of body tissue, and occurs when blood supply cannot reach a wound, causing it to rot and produce a foul-smelling gas *(p.52)*. It usually affects extremities such as toes, fingers and limbs.

How did they treat gangrene in the First World War?

The only effective treatment for gangrene was amputation of the affected body part, to prevent it spreading and ultimately causing the patient's death.

TREATMENTS IN THE FIRST WORLD WAR

New methods for new injuries

What medical treatments did they use in the First World War?

Doctors developed new treatments for the illnesses and injuries that were caused by the fighting and by the conditions in the trenches.

What medical treatments for wounded limbs were developed during the First World War?

There were many injuries to arms and legs in the First World War *(p.51)* - 240,000 soldiers lost limbs through amputation. New techniques were developed as a result:

- ☑ The Thomas splint *(p.58)* was used to keep injured legs still, while soldiers were being transported from the front.
- ☑ Lighter and more mobile prosthetic limbs were developed for amputees.

Which medical treatments were used to treat gas injuries in the First World War?

Around 186,000 British soldiers on the Western Front were affected by gas *(p.52)* injuries, but only around 2.6% of them died. There were different treatments for different gas injuries:

- ☑ Soldiers affected by chlorine and phosgene gas *(p.52)* needed oxygen, and were kept in hospital for up to two months.
- ☑ Mobile shower units were set up for soldiers affected by mustard gas *(p.52)*, as they had to wash with soap and water to prevent burns. Their eyes also needed bathing as soon as possible.

Which medical treatments were used to fight infections in the First World War?

During the First World War *(p.51)*, doctors developed a number of ways to prevent wounds becoming infected in the dirty conditions of the Western Front:

- ☑ Soldiers were given anti-tetanus serum to protect against tetanus.
- ☑ Wounds were washed in carbolic *(p.27)* lotion, an antiseptic *(p.29)* solution. Once the wounds were closed, they were wrapped in bandages soaked in carbolic acid *(p.27)*.
- ☑ Amputations were carried out to prevent life-threatening infections spreading through the bodies of the injured.
- ☑ Wound excision, or debridement, involved cutting dead tissue away from a wound to prevent infection.
- ☑ The Carrel-Dakin method *(p.58)* was a system of tubes that ensured a constant supply of sterilised salt solution to a wound.

What new medical treatments were developed in the First World War?

Doctors developed several new medical techniques and practices to deal with injuries in the First World War *(p.51)*. These included:

- ☑ The use of mobile X-ray *(p.43)* machines.
- ☑ Blood transfusions and blood banks.
- ☑ Brain surgery *(p.59)*.
- ☑ Plastic surgery *(p.58)*.

DID YOU KNOW?

The introduction of the Thomas splint made a huge difference to survival rates of wounded soldiers.

Before it was introduced, soldiers with compound fractures caused by bullet wounds to the leg only had a 20% chance of survival. By 1918, however, they had an 82% chance of survival.

THOMAS SPLINT

A splint for broken limbs

? What was the Thomas Splint?

The Thomas splint kept a wounded leg straight while the injured soldier was transported to a medical post. It reduced the death rate from compound fractures, from 80% to 18%.

DID YOU KNOW?

The Thomas Split is still used in hospitals today.

CARREL-DAKIN METHOD

A method to help prevent infections in wounds

? What was the Carrel-Dakin method?

The Carrel-Dakin method was a system of tubes that ensured a constant supply of sterilised salt solution to a wound, to prevent infection.

PLASTIC SURGERY IN THE FIRST WORLD WAR

Finding solutions for facial injuries

? What reasons were there for the development of plastic surgery in the First World War?

Some soldiers suffered horrific, disfiguring facial wounds. They often suffered psychological problems as a result of their appearance.

What treatment was available to disfigured soldiers at the start of WW1?

At the beginning of the war, the only solution was a mask made of tin.

Who was responsible for developing plastic surgery in the First World War?

Sir Harold Gillies *(p.60)*, an ear, nose and throat surgeon from New Zealand, pioneered several new techniques to improve the appearance of facial wounds.

What techniques did plastic surgeons use in the First World War?

The plastic surgeons of the First World War *(p.51)* developed a number of new techniques. These included:

☑ Pedicle tubes that were used to keep the blood flowing to skin grafts, to prevent the body from rejecting them.

☑ Bone and cartilage were used to make new facial features for soldiers who had suffered facial damage.

Where was plastic surgery developed in the First World War?

Queen's Hospital in Sidcup, Kent, was set up to care for soldiers with facial wounds. It was run by Sir Harold Gillies *(p.60)*.

How many soldiers underwent plastic surgery in the First World War?

By the end of the war, over 12,000 patients had undergone plastic surgery.

DID YOU KNOW?

About 16% of British soldiers who were discharged from the army had facial injuries.

Of these, one-third were classified as 'severe'.

BRAIN SURGERY IN THE FIRST WORLD WAR

New techniques for head injuries

What was the reason for the development of neurosurgery during the First World War?

The number of soldiers receiving brain injuries led to the development of neurosurgery thoughout the war.

What were the difficulties with neurosurgery during the First World War?

There were 2 main difficulties with neurosurgery in 1914:

☑ Head wounds affecting the brain were often fatal, because unconscious patients were difficult to move through the chain *(p.50)* of evacuation.

☑ Surgeons had little experience of neurosurgery.

Who developed neurosurgery during the First World War?

American neurosurgeon Harvey Cushing *(p.60)* used new techniques to treat brain injuries.

How was neurosurgery used to treat brain injuries in the First World War?

Two main methods were developed to deal with brain injuries:

☑ Magnets were used to remove metal fragments from the brain.

☑ Local anaesthetic *(p.22)* was used because it reduced swelling to the brain. General anaesthetic was found to increase swelling and therefore made brain surgery more dangerous.

What were the results of Harvey Cushing's work on neurosurgery during the First World War?

Cushing's *(p.60)* techniques improved the survival rate from brain surgery, from an average of 50% to 71%.

How did the Brodie helmet reduce the need for neurosurgery in the First World War?

In 1915, the Brodie helmet was introduced to help prevent head injuries. It was made from steel and had a strap to keep it on the soldier's head. It is estimated that it reduced the fatality of head wounds by 80%.

DID YOU KNOW?

Before Cushings innovations, brain surgery didn't have a high survival rate.

However, by 1917 Cushing had increased the survival rate of his patients from 50% to 71%.

HARVEY CUSHING

Father of Neurosurgery

Who was Harvey Cushing?

Harvey Cushing was an American neurosurgeon, who pioneered new brain surgery *(p.59)* techniques in the First World War *(p.51)*.

DID YOU KNOW?

Cushing was responsible for discovering the 'Cushing reflex'.

This was a way of explaining the relationship between blood pressure and intracranial pressure on the brain.

HAROLD GILLIES

A pioneer of plastic surgery

Who was Harold Gillies?

Harold Gillies was an ear, nose and throat specialist from New Zealand, who developed plastic surgery *(p.58)*. He pioneered several new techniques to improve the appearance of facial injuries in the First World War *(p.51)*.

X-RAYS IN THE FIRST WORLD WAR

Putting x-rays to work on the battlefield

Were X-rays used in the First World War?

X-rays were first invented in 1895, but they were put to more common use during the First World War *(p.51)*.

How were X-rays used in the First World War?

There were 2 main uses of X-rays in the First World War *(p.51)*:

☑ Before surgeons operated on patients with bullet and shrapnel injuries, two X-rays were taken of the wounds, so the surgeons knew exactly where the pieces were located.

☑ British Base Hospitals, and some Casualty Clearing Stations, had large X-ray *(p.43)* machines.

What were mobile X-ray units in the First World War?

There are 3 main things to note about mobile X-ray *(p.43)* machines:

☑ Pioneering radiologist, Marie Curie *(p.45)*, developed mobile X-ray *(p.43)* machines that could be transported in vans, and used at the Western Front.

☑ The RAMC *(p.64)* had six mobile X-ray *(p.43)* units on the Western Front.

☑ Mobile X-ray *(p.43)* units were set up in a tent at the back of a van, and powered by the van's engine.

What were the disadvantages of X-ray machines during the First World War?

The use of X-rays in the First World War *(p.51)* was problematic, particularly with the mobile units. There were 5 main problems.

☑ The radiation *(p.44)* from X-ray *(p.43)* machines could be harmful and cause burns.

☑ Pictures from mobile X-ray *(p.43)* machines were of poorer quality than those from the larger static machines. They were, however, usually good enough for the surgeons to work from.

☑ Soldiers had to remain still for a few minutes while the X-ray *(p.43)* was taken, even if they were in pain.

☑ The tubes of the X-ray *(p.43)* machine were fragile, and became too hot if the machine was used for more than an hour at a time.

☑ X-rays could only identify objects such as bullets and shrapnel. They could not identify fragments of clothing or soil in a wound.

DID YOU KNOW?

The original x-ray machines emitted 1,500 times as much radiation as they do today.

BLOOD TRANSFUSIONS IN THE FIRST WORLD WAR

Developing the storage and transfusion of blood

What about blood transfusions in the First World War?

In the late 19th century, blood transfusions were given person-to-person and often resulted in infection and death. By the end of the First World War *(p.51)*, however, medical advances had made them much safer and more common.

What new techniques were used for blood transfusion in the First World War?

Techniques used in blood transfusions developed throughout the war.

☑ In 1915, Lawrence Bruce Robertson (p.62) developed a method of transferring blood using a syringe and a tube, as person-to-person transfusions weren't practical on the Western Front.

☑ Also in 1915, Richard Weil (p.63) discovered that blood which had sodium nitrate added to it could be stored for up to 2 days if refrigerated.

☑ Geoffrey Keynes created a portable blood transfusion (p.30) kit, so that transfusions could be carried out near the frontline.

 How did blood banks help blood transfusions in the First World War?

By 1917, most casualty clearing stations used blood transfusions regularly. The building of depots for storing blood began before the Battle of Cambrai. This helped blood transfusion (p.30) as there was an available store of blood to use.

 How was infection prevented during blood transfusions in the First World War?

Before the war, many patients died from infections after blood transfusions. New discoveries prevented this happening:

☑ In 1900-1901, Austrian scientist Karl Landsteiner (p.31) discovered there were different blood types, which he named A, B, AB and O. This meant people were given the right blood, making transfusions safer.

☑ Aseptic surgery (p.29) practices prevented infection as a result of the transfusion process.

 How did they prevent blood for transfusions from clotting in the First World War?

One problem with storing blood was that it clotted and became thick and sticky. During the First World War (p.51), doctors needed to find ways to avoid this:

☑ In 1915, Richard Lewisohn (p.63) discovered that adding sodium citrate to blood prevented clotting for two days.

☑ In 1916, Francis Rous (p.63) and James Turner (p.63) extended the storage time of blood from 2 days to 4 weeks if it was refrigerated, by adding citrate glucose to stop it clotting.

DID YOU KNOW?

The blood group stored in the Cambrai blood bank was type O, which was safer to use with all blood groups.

LAWRENCE BRUCE ROBERTSON

A Canadian surgeon who served in the First World War.

↑

 Who was Lawrence Bruce Robertson?

Lawrence Bruce Robertson was a Canadian surgeon, who developed a method of transferring blood using a syringe and a tube.

RICHARD WEIL

American doctor in WWI

Who was Richard Weil?

Richard Weil was an American doctor. He discovered that blood could be kept fresh for up to 2 days, if it had sodium nitrate added to it and it was kept refridgerated.

RICHARD LEWISOHN

German-American surgeon

Who was Richard Lewisohn?

Richard Lewisohn was an American surgeon, who discovered that adding sodium citrate to blood prevented the blood from clotting for two days.

FRANCIS ROUS

American doctor

Who was Francis Rous?

Francis Rous was an American virologist. He worked with James Turner *(p.63)* to extend the storage time for blood, from 2 days to 4 weeks. They worked out that adding citrate glucose to the blood, and refrigerating it, would stop it from clotting.

JAMES TURNER

American doctor

Who was James Turner?

James Turner was an American doctor. He worked with Francis Rous *(p.63)* to extend the storage time for blood, from 2 days to 4 weeks. They worked out that adding citrate glucose to the blood, and refrigerating it, would stop it from clotting.

ROYAL ARMY MEDICAL CORPS

Doctors at the front

What was the Royal Army Medical Corps?

Doctors and medics in the army belonged to the Royal Army Medical Corps, or RAMC. They worked in different stations on the Western Front.

What was the chain of evacuation for the RAMC?

There was a 'chain *(p.50)* of evacuation' to get wounded soldiers to a safe treatment area. The links in the chain were:

- ✓ Regimental Aid Posts (RAP).
- ✓ Dressing stations (ADS and MDS).
- ✓ Casualty Clearing Stations (CCS).
- ✓ Base hospitals.

DID YOU KNOW?

The RAMC grew over the course of the First World War.

In 1914, there were 3,168 medical officers in the RAMC. By 1918 there were 13,061, and over 50% of all Britain's doctors had joined the army.

CASUALTY TRANSPORT IN THE FIRST WORLD WAR

Moving the wounded

What was transport like for wounded soldiers in the First World War?

It was important to move casualties away from the front line as quickly as possible but due to the nature of the fighting new methods were developed during the war.

How were the injured transported in the First World War?

There were 5 main forms of transport used for moving casualties.

- ✓ Stretcher bearers carried injured soldiers away from the front line. This was dangerous and difficult work.
- ✓ Initially, horse drawn carriages were used to move casualties. These were uncomfortable and could make injuries worse.
- ✓ Motor ambulances could move casualties to clearing stations. However, they often got stuck in the mud *(p.53)*.
- ✓ Once away from the front, casualties would be taken, by train or canal, to Base Hospitals on the coast.
- ✓ If necessary, casualties were placed on ships to be taken back to Britain.

Why was the transport of wounded soldiers from the battlefield difficult?

Removing casualties from the battlefield was difficult because roads had been destroyed, there were many shell holes, and the terrain was often very wet and muddy.

Quizzes, amazing exam preparation tools and more at GCSEHistory.com

NURSING IN THE FIRST WORLD WAR

Women on the Western Front

How did women get involved in nursing in ?

Thousands of women volunteered to become nurses - trained and untrained - during . Some were sent to France and Belgium to look after wounded soldiers.

What organisations could women join to become nurses in ?

There were 3 key organisations that women could join to become nurses in :

- ☑ Voluntary Aid Detachments (VADs), were <u>untrained nurses in</u> .
- ☑ The Queen Alexandra Imperial Military Nursing Service *(p.66)* (QAIMNS), consisted of <u>trained nurses</u>. QAIMNS was the largest group to work with the army during the War.
- ☑ The First Aid Nursing Yeomanry *(p.65)* (FANY) sent mobile units of volunteer nurses and <u>first aid</u> specialists to France.

FANY

First Aid Nursing Yeomanry

What was the First Aid Nursing Yeomanry?

The First Aid Nursing Yeomanry (FANY) sent mobile units of volunteer nurses and first aid specialists to France.

When was the First Aid Nursing Yeomanry founded?

It was founded in <u>1907.</u>

What did the First Aid Nursing Yeomanry do in the First World War?

In 1916, the British Army allowed FANY to <u>drive ambulances,</u> replacing the red cross drivers, and to give emergency first aid.

VAD

Untrained volunteer nurses

What were VADs?

Voluntary Aid Detachments (VADs), were <u>untrained nurses</u> in the First World War *(p.51)*. They were organised by the British Red Cross.

What was the role of the Voluntary Aid Detachments in the First World War?

The Voluntary Aid Detachments had 3 key roles in the First World War *(p.51)*:

- ☑ They nursed in RAMC *(p.64)* hospitals.
- ☑ They were untrained volunteers, who often performed simple cleaning tasks.
- ☑ They drove ambulances.

QAIMNS

The Queen Alexandra Imperial Medical Nursing Service

What was the Queen Alexandra Imperial Military Nursing Service?

The Queen Alexandra Imperial Military Nursing Service (QAIMNS), consisted of <u>trained nurses</u>. QAIMNS was the largest group to work with the army during the First World War *(p.51)*.

When was the Queen Alexandra Imperial Military Nursing Service created?

Queen Alexandra Imperial Military Nursing Service (QAIMNS) was created in <u>1902.</u>

How many nurses were in the Queen Alexandra Imperial Military Nursing Service?

At the start of the First World War *(p.51)* there were 300 nurses. By the end of the war there were around 10,000.

FEMALE DOCTORS IN THE FIRST WORLD WAR

Women doctors fight for the right to serve

Could women be doctors in the First World War?

The First World War *(p.51)* increased the demand for medical staff and created opportunities for female doctors.

Why were women doctors needed during The First World War?

50% of male doctors in Britain were called up to the RAMC *(p.64)*, and new hospitals were opened to treat the wounded.

How many women worked as doctors at the beginning of the First World War?

By 1914, only 1% of women were doctors. They could only work as GPs, or in hospitals for women and children.

Could women be doctors in the RAMC in the First World War?

In 1916, the army allowed women doctors to work with the RAMC *(p.64)* in Malta. However, unlike men, they did not automatically become officers.

What was the Women's Hospital Corps for doctors in the First World War?

Dr Flora Murray *(p.68)* and Dr Louisa Garrett Anderson *(p.68)* founded the Women's Hospital Corps to open female-run hospitals in France and London.

What was the effect of the First World War on women doctors?

Some of the effects of the First World War *(p.51)* on women doctors were:

- ☑ Even though 20% of female doctors worked in hospitals in the war, they were expected to return to their old roles as GPs when it ended.
- ☑ Twelve London teaching hospitals accepted women during the war. Afterwards, only the London Free Hospital continued to allow women to become students.
- ☑ The war is believed to have played a role in increasing the number of female doctors, from 610 in 1911 to 1,500 by 1921.

WOMEN AT THE FRONT IN THE FIRST WORLD WAR

Women find roles on the Front

Were there any women at the Front in the First World War?

Although the British Army did not want 'hysterical women' near the front lines, some women did work in medical roles at or near the Western Front.

What was the Women's Army Auxiliary Corps in the First World War?

When the Women's Army Auxiliary Corps was created in 1917, many women who joined worked as ambulance drivers.

How did women get to the Front in the First World War?

Some women, particularly wealthy ones, set up independent ambulance corps and travelled to France and Belgium. Mairi Chisholm and Elsie Knocker set up a first-aid post near the front lines.

Did women work in hospitals at the Front in the First World War?

Doctor Louisa Garrett and Doctor Flora Murray *(p.68)* founded the Women's Hospital Corps and opened hospitals in France. Mabel Stobart *(p.69)* founded a female-run hospital in Belgium.

DID YOU KNOW?

Mairi Chisholm and Elsie Knocker were named 'the Madonnas of Pervyse' by the British press.

DR LOUISA GARRETT ANDERSON

Suffragette and political reformer

Who was Dr Louisa Garrett Anderson?

Dr Louisa Garrett Anderson founded the Women's Hospital Corps to open female-run hospitals in France and London.

DR FLORA MURRAY

Suffragette and political reformer

Who was Dr Flora Murray?

Dr Flora Murray founded the Women's Hospital Corps to open female-run hospitals in France and London.

MABEL STOBART

A suffragist and aid worker in the Balkan Wars and during the First World War.

Who was Mabel Stobart?

Mabel Stobart founded a female-run hospital in Belgium. She created and commanded all female-led medical units in WWI *(p.51)*. She held the rank of Major.

SECOND WORLD WAR MEDICINE

Another war means more challenges in medicine.

How did the Second World War change medicine?

The Second World War and its resulting injuries drove further developments in the world of medicine. There were particular advances in the areas of blood transfusions and skin grafts.

Who were the pioneering surgeons of the Second World War medicine?

Some famous surgeons in the Second World War were a British neurosurgeon called Wylie McKissock *(p.71)*, an American heart surgeon named Dwight Harken, and Archibald McIndoe *(p.71)*, a plastic surgeon from New Zealand.

What role did women play in medicine during the Second World War?

The Second World War opened up opportunities for women to work in new roles, although fewer male doctors were called up than in the First World War *(p.51)*.

- ☑ Women worked as ambulance drivers, stretcher-bearers, and with the rescue services during air raids.
- ☑ Nurses were given military ranks from 1941, and had to take part in physical training after 1943. Many members of the Queen Alexandra Imperial Military Nursing Service *(p.66)* (QAIMNS) served overseas.
- ☑ Members of the QAIMNS landed on the beaches of Normandy after D-Day in June 1944.
- ☑ More women studied medicine in 1946 than in 1938. In 1938, there were approximately 2,000 female medical students, which rose by 900 in 1946. Women doctors were more likely to work in hospitals.
- ☑ Children that were to be evacuated received a medical inspection by district nurses.

DID YOU KNOW?

Second World War battle injuries were different from those in the First World War, because of the different technology in use.

Whereas soldiers in the First World War were more at risk from bullets and shrapnel, those in the Second World War were more likely to suffer burns injuries.

PLASTIC SURGERY IN THE SECOND WORLD WAR

Medical treatments continue to develop

What was the reason for plastic surgery developing during the Second World War?

The increased use of machinery such as aircraft and tanks meant that <u>burn injuries</u> were more common. Surgeons therefore developed new methods to treat them effectively.

What better methods of plastic surgery were developed to treat burns victims in WW2?

Surgeons developed new and better methods of plastic surgery *(p.58)* to treat burns victims:

☑ <u>Saline, instead</u> of chemicals, was used to treat burns, which improved movement in the area when the burn had healed.

☑ The war led to new advances in <u>skin graft me</u>thods by transfering healthy skin to an injured area.

☑ Penicillin *(p.49)* was used to prevent infection when treating burns victims.

DID YOU KNOW?

Archibald McIndoe's patients called themselves 'the Guinea Pig Club'.

They were given psychological support to adjust to their experiences and injuries. By the end of the war, the club had 643 members.

PSYCHOLOGICAL TREATMENT IN THE SECOND WORLD WAR

Improved attitudes to mental health since the First World War

How did they treat PTSD in the Second World War?

In the Second World War, psychological problems were often known as battle fatigue. Understanding of the psychological impact of warfare had improved by the Second World War, and 18 psychiatric hospitals were set up in peaceful surroundings.

BLOOD TRANSFUSIONS IN THE SECOND WORLD WAR

Blood transfusions become better and more widespread

What developments were there in blood transfusions in the Second World War?

During the Second World War, blood transfusion *(p.30)* became more common and more effective due to a number of new developments.

What were the key developments in blood transfusion during the Second World War?

There were 4 key developments in blood transfusions:

☑ <u>Blood donations became</u> more common. Around 700,000 people gave blood during the Second World War.

☑ There were <u>better facilities for storing</u> blood, such as the Army Blood Supply Depot located in Bristol.

- Doctors began to use blood plasma for transfusions and developed a dried plasma package which was easier to store and transport *(p.64)*.
- In 1939, the discovery of the rhesus blood group, and work on the tetanus vaccination, meant blood transfusions became safer.

WYLIE MCKISSOCK

Pioneering Second World War brain surgeon

Who was Wylie McKissock?

Wylie McKissock was a British neurosurgeon who studied new techniques and worked on brain injuries during the Second World War, building on the work of Harvey Cushing *(p.60)* in the First World War *(p.51)*.

DWIGHT HARKEN

The Father of Cardiac Surgery

Who was Dwight Harken?

Dwight Harken was an American surgeon who developed a new technique for removing bullets and shrapnel from the heart. During the Second World War, he conducted 130 of these operations, with not a single one of them resulting in death.

ARCHIBALD MCINDOE

Pioneering plastic surgeon and founder of the 'Guinea Pig Club'

Who was Archibald McIndoe?

Archibald McIndoe was a plastic surgeon from New Zealand who worked as an RAF consultant surgeon, pioneering new treatments for burns. He was related to Harold Gillies *(p.60)*, the First World War *(p.51)* plastic surgeon.

WELFARE STATE

'From the cradle to the grave'

What was the purpose of the Welfare State?

After the Second World War, British Prime Minister Clement Attlee and his Labour government set up the welfare state to provide care for everyone, 'from the cradle to the grave'.

How did the Second World War contribute to the creation of the Welfare State?

The Second World War helped to bring about the creation of the Welfare State in 3 key ways.

- ☑ The war forced Britain to deal with large numbers of injuries.
- ☑ The war expanded the role of the government in health, with the Emergency Medical Service.
- ☑ People were shocked at the state of the hygiene and health of some of the evacuees.

What new measures did the Labour government introduce under the Welfare State?

The Labour government introduced 3 main reforms after 1945 that affected health.

- ☑ The New Towns Act of 1946 was introduced, to plan new towns.
- ☑ The National Insurance Act of 1946 provided better unemployment and sick pay, maternity benefits, and improved old age pensions.
- ☑ The National Health Service *(p.74)* was launched in 1948, which provided free healthcare at the point of delivery and was paid for by taxes.

DID YOU KNOW?

The Welfare State was mostly supported. However, some people objected to it.

The Welfare State was opposed by some groups of people. Some were afraid that taxes would increase and some believed that it would discourage people from looking for jobs. They feared that people might 'live off the state'.

CLEMENT ATTLEE

Prime minister of the Labour government responsible for the Welfare State

Who was Clement Attlee?

Clement Attlee was a Labour politician who served as prime minister of the United Kingdom from 1945 to 1951.

What were Clement Attlee's beliefs?

Attlee had left-wing beliefs and his government is most famous for creating the NHS *(p.74)*. Attlee supported the Marshall Plan and promoted a NATO military alliance against the USSR and its satellite states.

What conferences did Clement Attlee attend?

Attlee attended the Potsdam Conference in July 1945, to discuss Nazi Germany and how to end the war.

WILLIAM BEVERIDGE
Liberal politician and social reformer

Who was William Beveridge?

William Beveridge was a government minister, who wrote a report about rebuilding Britain after the Second World War.

When was the Beveridge Report published?

William Beveridge published The Beveridge Report in 1942.

What problems in society did Beveridge suggest the government should tackle?

The Beveridge Report suggested the government had a role to play in tackling the 5 'giant evils' of British society:

- ☑ Want (poverty).
- ☑ Disease.
- ☑ Ignorance (lack of education).
- ☑ Squalor (unhygienic living conditions).
- ☑ Idleness (unemployment).

What was the significance of the Beveridge Report?

The Beveridge Report became very famous, and raised people's hopes that the government would do more to build a healthier society after the Second World War. It formed the basis of the welfare state. *(p.72)*

How did the governement respond to the Beveridge Report?

The government took 5 key measures to fix the 5 'giant evils'.

- ☑ The government introduced a range of benefits. For example a weekly family allowance, paid to the mother.
- ☑ The NHS *(p.74)* was created.
- ☑ The Clean Air Acts (1952 & 1956) aimed to reduce pollution in towns and cities.
- ☑ The government embarked on a slum clearance programme in the 1960s. They were replaced by council housing with modern conveniences such as central heating.
- ☑ New towns, such as Milton Keynes, were built from scratch with more space and better public facilities like parks.

NATIONAL HEALTH SERVICE
'The NHS will last as long as there are folk left with the faith to fight for it' Anuerin Bevan

What was the NHS?
The National Health Service (NHS) was set up to provide free healthcare to patients at the point of delivery.

Who was responsible for establishing the NHS?
Aneurin Bevan *(p.75)* was a Labour Minister for Health from Wales, who was responsible for setting up the NHS.

Why was the NHS introduced?
By the end of the Second World War, changes to society meant that the idea of a public health service was much more popular, for 5 key reasons.

- ☑ Many children were evacuated to the country during the Second World War. People were horrified by the poverty that they saw.
- ☑ By the mid-twentieth century, people had become more used to the idea of the government playing a role in people's lives.
- ☑ Advances in medicine meant that there were more ways to help the sick.
- ☑ The Second World War had already forced the government to organise, and take more control of, hospitals and medical services.
- ☑ The Beveridge *(p.73)* Report of 1942 inspired the creation of the NHS.

When did the NHS begin?
The NHS was founded on 5th July, 1948.

Who opposed the creation of the NHS?
There were 2 main areas of opposition to the creation of the NHS.

- ☑ Some doctors opposed the introduction of the NHS because it reduced their income from private patients. Bevan *(p.75)* promised they could continue to work privately, as well as receiving a salary from the government.
- ☑ Many Conservatives disliked the NHS because of the burden on the taxpayer, but it was too popular with the general public to be abolished.

How was the NHS organised?
The NHS was organised in the following ways:

- ☑ Hospitals were controlled by 14 regional boards, but were made part of a single system.
- ☑ Doctors, as well as dentists, pharmacists and opticians, had individual contracts with the NHS.
- ☑ GPs played an important role in providing primary health care, by diagnosing and treating patients, by referring them to hospital where necessary, or writing prescriptions for medicine.
- ☑ Local health authorities had responsibility for vaccination programmes, maternal and child welfare, health visitors, and school dental services. They were led by a medical officer.

What services does the NHS provide?
The NHS provides services through medical treatment, hospitals, specialist healthcare professionals, preventative healthcare, and care for the vulnerable.

- ☑ The NHS provides treatment for illness and injury, including surgery, blood transfusions and medication.
- ☑ The NHS runs hospitals, provides ambulance services to transport *(p.64)* patients to them, and accident and emergency care.

Quizzes, amazing exam preparation tools and more at GCSEHistory.com

- [x] The NHS provides access to healthcare professionals and services such as GPs, mental health services, dental treatment, and opticians.
- [x] The NHS works to prevent illness to cut down on the cost of treatment. This includes campaigns to encourage healthier lifestyles, vaccinations, and diagnostic screening.
- [x] The NHS provides care for the vulnerable, such as the elderly and disabled. Maternity care and health visitors are provided for mothers and new babies.

In what ways has the NHS been successful?

The NHS has been successful in improving healthcare in Britain in 6 main ways.

- [x] The NHS has improved hospitals and healthcare facilities.
- [x] The NHS has led to a fall in child mortality rates.
- [x] The NHS has implemented a national vaccination scheme, eradicating many diseases.
- [x] The NHS provides free healthcare for all, regardless of their ability to pay.
- [x] The NHS has raised life expectancy.
- [x] The NHS lowers treatment costs by promoting preventive health care.

How much did the NHS cost?

The NHS was paid for by National Insurance contributions and taxes. In 1948, it cost £12.9 billion.

How much did the NHS raise life expectancy?

In 1930, on average, men lived until the age of 58 and women until 62. By 1950, this had increased to 66 for men and 70 for women.

What happened to the NHS in the 1960s?

During the 1960s, the government built more hospitals across the country, and introduced a GP's charter in 1966, which improved standards in care.

DID YOU KNOW?

In 2020, the NHS was the fifth largest employer in the world.

ANEURIN BEVAN

The founder of the NHS

Who was Aneurin Bevan?

Aneurin Bevan was a Labour minister from Wales, who was responsible for setting up the NHS *(p.74)* in 1948.

A

Abolish, Abolished - to stop something, or get rid of it.

Alliance - a union between groups or countries that benefits each member.

Amputate, Amputation - to surgically remove a limb from someone's body.

Anaesthetic - a drug used in surgery to remove pain by causing a temporary loss of sensation or awareness.

Anatomy - the study of how the body is made up internally, what it looks like, how it is structured and how the different parts are positioned.

Antibiotics - microbes that can kill germs that cause diseases.

Antiseptic - a substance that kills harmful bacteria to prevent infection.

Artillery - large guns used in warfare.

Aseptic - an absence of germs and harmful bacteria; surgically sterile.

B

Bacteria, Bacterium - a microorganism that causes diseases.

Bacteriology - the study of bacteria.

Bile, Black bile - one of the four 'humours' in medieval medicine. A black substance observed in excrement and vomit, it probably constituted clotted blood.

Blood group - refers to the type of blood someone has and used to distinguish between different types for blood transfusions.

Blood transfusion - the process of giving a patient blood from a donor.

C

Campaign - a political movement to get something changed; in military terms, it refers to a series of operations to achieve a goal.

Casualties - people who have been injured or killed, such as during a war, accident or catastrophe.

Catgut - a material made from the dried, twisted intestines of sheep or horses and used as a ligature.

Cesspit - a hole which has been dug to store sewage and waste.

Charter - a legal written grant, issued by a monarch or country's legislative power, permitting certain rights or privileges.

Choler - pus or stomach acid found in vomit. It was one of the four 'humours' in medieval medicine.

Circulation, Circulatory - the movement of blood around the body, pumped by the heart.

Civil servant - a person who works for the government, either at national or local level.

Conference - a formal meeting to discuss common issues of interest or concern.

Contagious - something that spreads from one person or organism to another, usually referring to illness or disease.

Council - an advisory or administrative body set up to manage the affairs of a place or organisation. The Council of the League of Nations contained the organisation's most powerful members.

Culture - the ideas, customs, and social behaviour of a particular people or society.

D

Diagnose - to work out the nature or type of a disease, illness or medical condition by looking at the symptoms.

Diphtheria - a serious bacterial infection that can lead to breathing difficulties, heart failure, paralysis and even death. It mainly affects children.

Dissection - the careful and methodical cutting apart of a body or plant to inspect its structure.

E

Empire - a group of states or countries ruled over and controlled by a single monarch.

Epidemic - an outbreak of disease that spreads quickly and affects many individuals at the same time.

Eradicate, Eradication - to destroy something and completely wipe it out.

Extreme - furthest from the centre or any given point. If someone holds extreme views, they are not moderate and are considered radical.

F

Fasting - to deliberately refrain from eating, and often drinking, for a period of time.

Fatalities, Fatality - Deaths.

Front - in war, the area where fighting is taking place.

G

Gangrene - the death of body tissue due to either lack of blood or serious bacterial infection.

General anaesthetic - a state of controlled unconsciousness using drugs, usually during surgery so the patient can not feel any pain or move.

Germ - microorganisms that can cause disease. The name was coined by Louis Pasteur as he saw them germinating.

H

Hygiene, Hygienic - a term for conditions or practices with the aim of maintaining good health and preventing disease, especially in regard to cleanliness.

I

Iatrochemistry - a branch of both chemistry and medicine, seeking chemical solutions to disease and illness, popular during the 16th and 17th centuries.

Independence, Independent - to be free of control, often meaning by another country, allowing the people of a nation the ability to govern themselves.

Industrial - related to industry, manufacturing and/or production.

Industrialisation, Industrialise, Industrialised - the process of developing industry in a country or region where previously there was little or none.

Industry - the part of the economy concerned with turning raw materials into into manufactured goods, for example making furniture from wood.

Infection - the result of disease-causing microorganisms finding their way into a wound or suitable body tissue and multiplying.

L

Laissez-faire - the idea a government should take a hands-off approach to matters such as public health or the free market; it translates from the French as 'let it be'.

Liberal - politically, someone who believes in allowing personal freedom without too much control by the government or state.

Ligature - something used to tie or bind tightly; an example in medical use is around a limb to slow bleeding from a wound.

Limb - an arm or leg.

Local anaesthetic - a way to numb an isolated part of the body using medication, for example to prevent pain during minor surgery or stop an injury hurting.

M

Magic bullet - a chemical compound that will kill a specific germ without harming other cells.

Malnutrition - lack of proper nutrition caused by not eating enough of the right things or not having enough to eat. It can also be caused by the body not being able to use the food that is eaten.

Mass - an act of worship in the Catholic Church.

Medic - someone who has medical knowledge but is not a doctor.

Medical chemistry - a branch of both chemistry and medicine, seeking chemical solutions to disease and illness, popular during the 16th and 17th centuries.

Medieval era, Medieval times, Middle Ages - the period from circa 1250 to 1500.

Miasma, Miasma theory, Miasmata - the theory that diseases were caused by a bad air.

Microbe - a living organism that can only be seen through a microscope.

Minister - a senior member of government, usually responsible for a particular area such as education or finance.

Mortality, Mortality rates - refers to death; the mortality rate shows how many people are dying in a society.

N

Neurosurgeon - a surgeon who specialises in neurosurgery.

Neurosurgery - the medical specialism concerned with the diagnosis and treatment of injuries to the brain, spinal cord and spinal column.

No man's land - the land between the opposing sides' trenches in the First World War.

P

Pharmaceutical - relating to medicinal drugs, the industry that manufactures them, and their preparation, use or sale.

Phlegm - the thick liquid produced by the mucous membranes, usually coughed or sneezed out during illness.

Physician - someone qualified to practise medicine, often used as another name for a doctor.

Pioneer - the first person to explore or settle in a new area.

Poverty - the state of being extremely poor.

Prevent, Preventative, Preventive - steps taken to stop something from happening.

Printing press - a machine that reproduces writing and images by using ink on paper, making many identical copies.

Production - a term used to describe how much of something is made, for example saying a factory has a high production rate.

Prosthetic, Prosthetic limb - an artificial body part.

Provision - the act of providing or supplying something for someone.

Psychological - referring to a person's mental or emotional state.

R

Raid - a quick surprise attack on the enemy.

Rational - when something is based on reason or logic, like science.

Reform, Reforming - change, usually in order to improve an institution or practice.

Revolution - the forced overthrow of a government or social system by its own people.

S

Satellite state - a country under the control of another, such as countries under USSR control during the Cold War.

Sepsis, Septicaemia - life-threatening and potentially fatal blood poisoning, where an existing infection triggers a chain reaction throughout the body.

Shrapnel - small pieces of metal from exploding shells or bombs which caused injuries to soldiers.

Skin grafts - a surgical procedure that involves removing healthy skin from one part of the body and transplanting it to a different area.

Splint - a strong, straight device used to protect and support a broken limb, keeping it in place.

Spontaneous generation - the theory that rotting material, for example food and excrement, created disease.

State, States - an area of land or a territory ruled by one government.

Sterilisation, Sterilise - to clean something so it is free of bacteria; also refers to a medical procedure that prevents a person from being able to reproduce.

Supernatural - an unscientific explanation for an event or manifestation unattributable to the laws of nature.

Symptom - an indication of something, such as a sign of a particular illness.

Syphilis - a bacterial infection usually transmitted through sexual contact.

T

Terrain - a stretch of land and usually used to refer to its physical features, eg mountainous, jungle etc.

Territories, Territory - an area of land under the control of a ruler/ country.

Transfusion - the process of transferring donated blood to a patient.

V

Vaccination, Vaccine - from the Latin 'vacca', meaning cow. Originally it referred to giving a person cowpox to prevent smallpox, but is now used for all methods of introducing a weak strain of a disease as a way of building immunity.

W

Ward, Wards - A ward is someone who is taken under the protection and power of someone else, usually because it is believed that they do not have the capacity to know what is best for them.

Welfare - wellbeing; often refers to money and services given to the poorest people.

Workhouse - a place for poor people who were unable to work or support themselves.

Y

Yellow bile - pus or stomach acid found in vomit. It was one of the four 'humours' in medieval medicine.

Quizzes, amazing exam preparation tools and more at GCSEHistory.com

Lightning Source UK Ltd.
Milton Keynes UK
UKHW052312231020
372132UK00003B/68

9 781913 887155